W9-BEG-786

New York

STATE ACTIVITY BOOK

GRADE 4

PUBLIC SCHOOL 262
500 MACON STREET
BROOKLYN, N. Y. 11233

HARCOURT BRACE & COMPANY

Orlando Atlanta Austin Boston San Francisco Chicago Dallas

New York Toronto London

Visit The Learning Site at http://www.hbschool.com

REVIEWERS AND CONSULTANTS

Joan Andrejko
Teacher—New York Geographic
    Consultant
Cohoes Middle School
Cohoes, New York

Christopher Clarity
Teacher
Public School 15
Brooklyn, New York

Sheila E. Conley
Associate Superintendent—
    Curriculum
Diocese of Brooklyn
Brooklyn, New York

Beverly Cowan
Teacher
Northside Elementary School
Levittown, New York

Dr. Peter Eisenstadt
Editor
The Encyclopedia of
    New York State
Rochester, New York

Howard M. Itkin
Teacher
Klem Road South Elementary
    School
Webster, New York

Paulette Johnson
Literacy Staff Developer
Public School 197
New York, New York

Dr. Carol Kammen
Tompkins County
Historian and Senior Lecturer
Department of History
Cornell University
Ithaca, New York

Nancy Maresca, Ed.D
Principal
Woodland Elementary School
East Syracuse, New York

Barbara O'Connor
Teacher
Phillip Schuyler Elementary
    School
Albany, New York

Dr. Jon Sterngass
Assistant Professor
Union College
Schenectady, New York

Vera Weiss
Teacher
Glen Worden Elementary School
Scotia, New York

Christine Zidik
Teacher
John F. Kennedy Magnet School
Port Chester, New York

Copyright © by Harcourt, Inc.

All rights reserved. No part of this publication may be reproduced or transmitted in any form or by any means, electronic or mechanical, including photocopy, recording, or any information storage and retrieval system, without permission in writing from the publisher.

Requests for permission to make copies of any part of the work should be mailed to the following address: School Permissions, Harcourt, Inc., 6277 Sea Harbor Drive, Orlando, Florida 32887-6777.

HARCOURT and the Harcourt Logo are trademarks of Harcourt, Inc.

For permission to reprint copyrighted material, grateful acknowledgment is made to the following sources:

Chelsea House Publishers, LLC.: "Little Red [Quail]" by the Yaqui from Literatures of the American Indian by A. LaVonne Brown Ruoff, edited by Frank W. Porter III. Copyright © 1991 by Chelsea House Publishers, a division of Main Line Book Co.

World Publications Group, Inc.: "We Are the Stars Which Sing" by the Algonquian from The Native Americans: An Illustrated History by David Hurst Thomas, edited by Betty Ballantine and Ian Ballantine. Published by Turner Publishing, 1993.

Photo credits appear at the back of this book.

Printed in the United States of America

ISBN 0-15-321559-3

4 5 6 7 8 9 10 073 10 09 08 07 06 05 04 03 02

CONTENTS

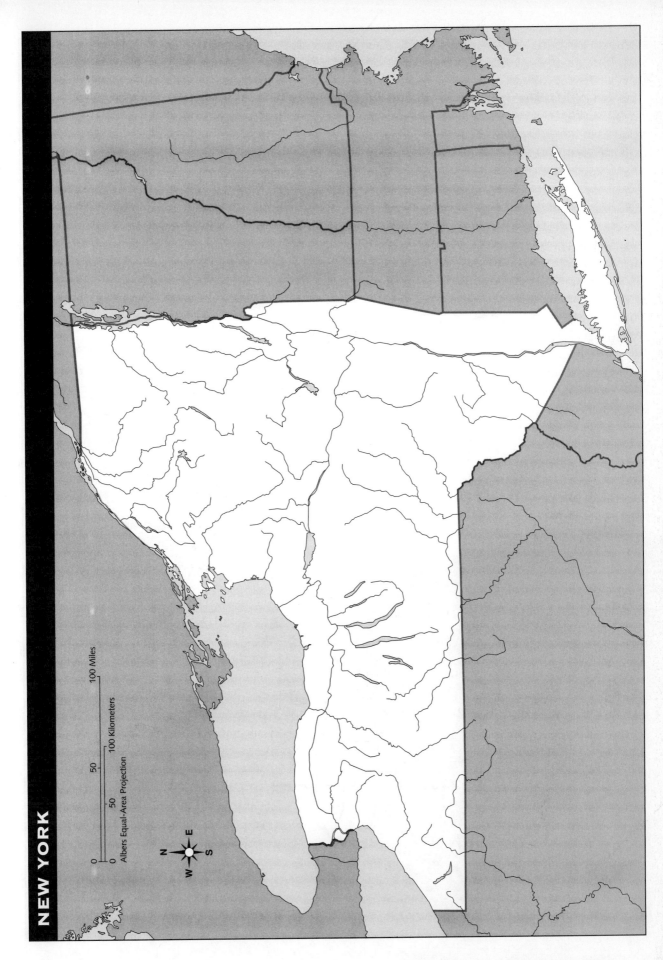

Harcourt Brace School Publishers

NEW YORK

100 Miles

100 Kilometers

50

50

0

0

Albers Equal-Area Projection

N
W · E
S

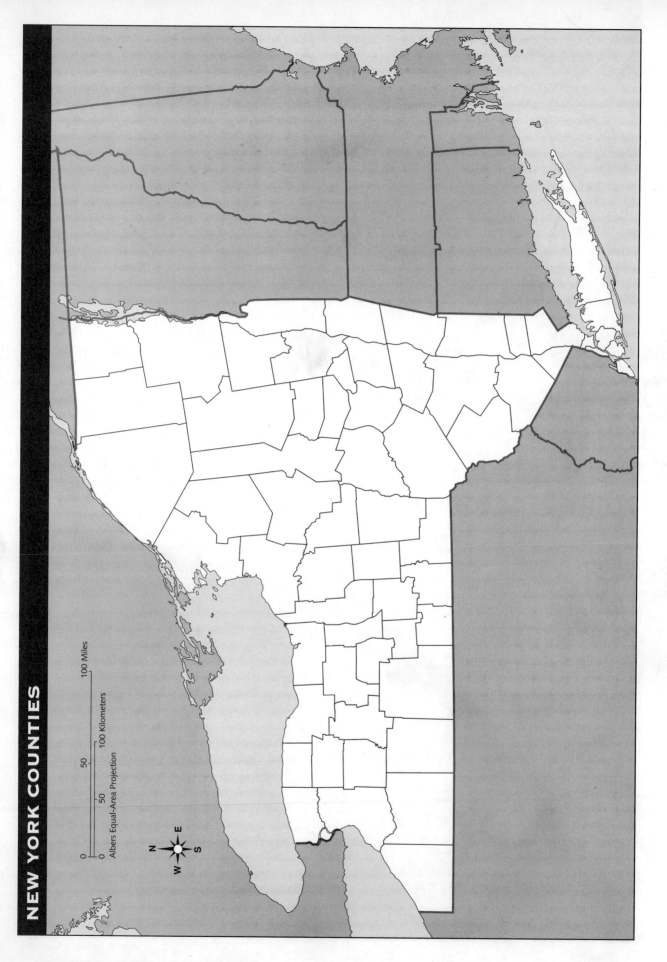

NEW YORK COUNTIES

100 Miles

50

50

0

0

100 Kilometers

Albers Equal-Area Projection

N
E
W
S

Harcourt Brace School Publishers

Introduction

Native Americans in New York State

Up until about 10,000 years ago, much of North America experienced times of freezing cold. Large sheets of ice, called **glaciers,** covered almost all the continent. These periods of time are known as the **Ice Ages.** In time, the Earth's temperature increased, and the glaciers began to melt. This allowed people to live in the once frozen areas.

Around 7000 B.C. the first people moved into what is today New York State. This age is known as the Paleo-Indian period. The Paleo-Indians were **nomads**, or people who move from place to place to find food. They hunted animals and gathered nuts and berries to eat.

Next came the Archaic (ar•KAY•ik) period that lasted from about 3500 B.C. to 1000 B.C. The people known today as Native Americans, or American Indians, began to live in the area of New York State during this time. The Native Americans were more settled than their Paleo-Indian **ancestors**— relatives who lived longer ago than grandparents. Like their ancestors, they also gathered plants and hunted animals. The Native Americans made new kinds of tools by sharpening stones, which they used to cut down trees for wood.

The Archaic period gave way to the Woodland period. During this time, Native Americans lived in more permanent settlements, or **villages**. They made clay pottery and learned to grow crops, becoming the first farmers on the land now known as New York.

When people from Europe, or Europeans, arrived in North America in the 1500s, most of the Native Americans living in New York State belonged to one of two larger groups. One of these groups spoke Algonquian (al•GAHN•kwee•uhn) Indian languages. The other group spoke a number of different languages that had some similar-sounding words. French explorers called these people the Iroquois (IR•uh•kwoy). Within these two larger groups were many smaller groups known as nations.

Anthropologists, or scientists who study groups of people, think that Algonquian-speaking tribes lived all along the North Atlantic coast. Some Algonquian nations lived in the Hudson River valley and the Mohawk River valley. Other Algonquian nations could be found in what is now New Jersey, Delaware, Virginia, and southeastern Canada. The main Algonquian nations were the Mahican (muh•HEE•kun), Abenaki (A•buh•nah•kee), Delaware (DEH•luh•wair), Wappinger (WAH•pin•jer), Munsee (MUHN•see), and Montauk (MAHN•tawk).

All the Algonquian nations had migrated to New York State about 1000 B.C. They came from what is now New England and Nova Scotia.

The native people whom the French called the Iroquois came to the New York area from farther west sometime between A.D. 1200 and A.D. 1300. The Native American nations of this group were the Mohawk (MOH•hawk), Oneida (oh•NY•duh), Onondaga (AH•nuhn•dahg•uh), Cayuga (kay•YOO•guh), Erie (IR•ee),

(continued)

Harcourt Brace School Publishers

Susquehanna (suhs•kwuh•HA•nuh), and Seneca (SEN•ih•kuh).

The Mohawk, Oneida, Onondaga, Cayuga, and Seneca nations all lived close together. The Erie and the Susquehanna lived farther west. For many years the five neighboring nations constantly battled one another.

Then, according to Onondaga history, two great leaders, Dekanawida (deh•kahn•uh•WIH•duh) and Hiawatha (hy•uh• WAH•thuh), convinced the warring nations to stop fighting and adopt the Great Law of Peace. At first, Onondaga leader Tadodaho (tuh•doh•DAH•hoh) did not support the law. In time, Dekanawida and Hiawatha convinced him to accept it.

As a result of the Great Law of Peace, the nations agreed to stop fighting and unite, forming the Five Nations. The people of the Five Nations called themselves the Haudenosaunee (hoh•DEE•noh•shoh•nee), which means the People of the Longhouse. The main purpose of uniting was to bring the Five Nations together so that they could defend their lands against attacks from other Native American groups.

Haudenosaunee Symbol of Unity

In 1714 the Haudenosaunee people added a sixth nation. This nation was the Tuscarora (tuhs•kuh•ROHR•uh). The Tuscaroras had traveled north because European settlers forced them from their lands in what is now North Carolina. Then the Haudenosaunee nations were known as the Six Nations.

In time, the Haudenosaunee people and new European settlers pushed most of the other Indian groups out of the area. By the end of the 1700s, the Haudenosaunee people were the only Native American group living in what would become New York State.

Review

CHECK UNDERSTANDING

1. What three periods of Native American settlement took place before the arrival of Europeans?
2. What was the main purpose of the Five Nations joining together?

THINK CRITICALLY

3. What might have been some of the benefits and drawbacks to membership in the Five Nations?

SHOW WHAT YOU KNOW

Find out more about the Haudenosaunee, or Iroquois, nations. Then on a separate sheet of paper, draw your own symbol for the Five Nations. Your symbol should express the ideas behind the Great Law of Peace and include references to all the member nations.

Harcourt Brace School Publishers

Activity

Native American Settlements

This map shows where Native Americans lived long ago in what is now New York State. The map legend tells you how to find the Algonquian and Haudenosaunee nations on the map.

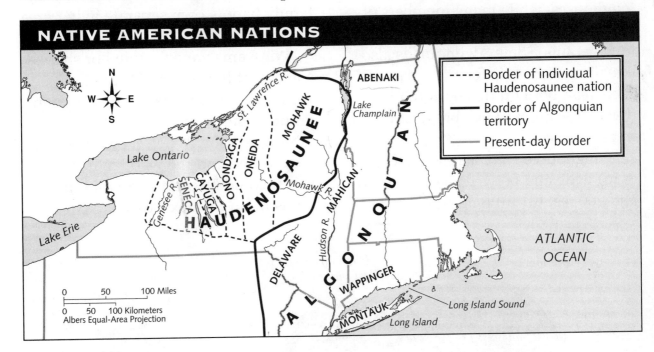

DIRECTIONS: Use the information on the map to answer the questions that follow.

1. According to the map, which three Haudenosaunee nations lived alongside Lake Ontario? _____

2. The Haudenosaunee nation that lived farthest west was called the Keepers of the Western Door. Which nation was that? _____

3. Which Haudenosaunee nation could have been called the Keepers of the Eastern Door? _____

4. Which Native American nation lived on what is now known as Long Island? Was that group part of the Algonquian or Haudenosaunee people?

   _____

   _____

5. Many of New York's Native Americans used canoes to travel. Use a pen or colored pencil to trace a water route on the map that a Mahican might have taken to get to Oneida territory.

Harcourt Brace School Publishers

Native American Houses

Each Native American group built different kinds of houses. People of the Haudenosaunee nations lived in longhouses, while many members of the Algonquian nations chose to live in wigwams. Some Algonquians also lived in longhouses for all or part of each year. Both groups built their dwellings out of wood, birchbark, and tree branches.

Longhouses were about 25 feet (8 m) wide and between 60 feet (18 m) and 200 feet (61 m) long—or about the size of four school buses wide and six school buses long. Ten or twelve families lived in one longhouse. Each family had its own separate living area and cooking fire.

Wigwams were rounded or shaped somewhat like a loaf of bread and were easy to build. Some Algonquian groups built wigwams for the winter hunting season. When they moved on, they left behind the wooden frame so that it could be used to rebuild the wigwam in the next season.

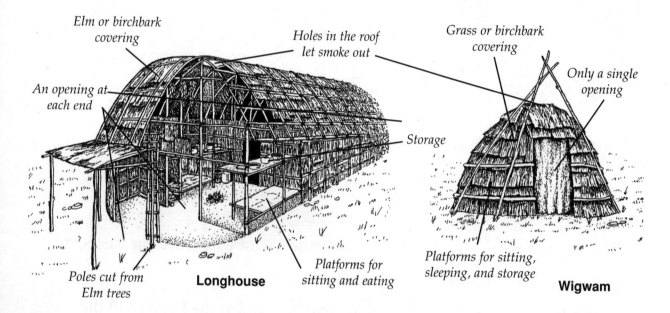

Longhouse labels: Elm or birchbark covering · Holes in the roof let smoke out · An opening at each end · Storage · Poles cut from Elm trees · Platforms for sitting and eating — **Longhouse**

Wigwam labels: Grass or birchbark covering · Only a single opening · Platforms for sitting, sleeping, and storage — **Wigwam**

DIRECTIONS: Study the pictures of the longhouse and the wigwam. How are these two kinds of houses similar and different? How are they similar to and different from your house? On a separate sheet of paper, write several paragraphs that compare the longhouse and the wigwam. Talk about what each house is made of, the kinds of openings each has, and the kinds of seating, sleeping, and storage areas found in each. Then, write several paragraphs that describe how a longhouse or wigwam is different from a house built today.

Harcourt Brace School Publishers

Native American Settlements and Your Community

The map on the next page shows early Native American settlements in New York State. Native Americans moved often, so only about 70 or 80 of these sites were ever used at the same time.

Haudenosaunee village

DIRECTIONS: Use the map on page 12 to learn about past Native American settlements near your community. First study the map. Then complete the activities below.

1. Put a star on the map to show the location of your community.

2. About how far was the nearest Native American settlement from where your community is today?

   _____

3. Why do you think so many Native American settlements were near water?

   _____

   _____

   _____

4. Think of a place near your community that the Haudenosaunee people might have settled. On a separate sheet of paper, describe the place and tell why you think it is a good spot. What advantages does it have? What disadvantages might it have?

Harcourt Brace School Publishers

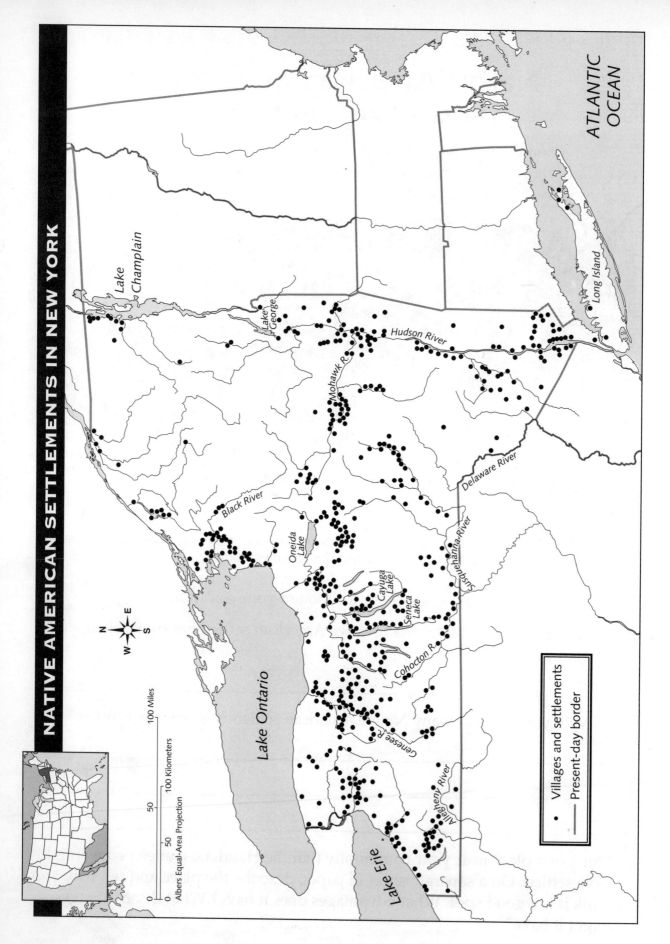

NATIVE AMERICAN SETTLEMENTS IN NEW YORK

ATLANTIC OCEAN

Long Island

Lake Champlain

Lake George

Hudson River

Mohawk R.

Delaware River

Black River

Oneida Lake

Susquehanna River

Cayuga Lake

Seneca Lake

Cohocton R.

Lake Ontario

Genesee R.

Allegheny River

Lake Erie

N E S W

100 Miles
50
100 Kilometers
50
0
Albers Equal-Area Projection

Villages and settlements
Present-day border

Harcourt Brace School Publishers

The Native American Way of Life

The geography of New York made it an ideal place for Native American life. Its climate of warm summers, cold winters, and enough rain allowed for good farming. The forests and river valleys provided important **natural resources,** or things in nature that people use, such as trees, animals, and water.

Both major Indian groups of New York, the Algonquian-speaking people and the Haudenosaunee people, led similar ways of life. Both groups lived in fort-like villages. They relied on the land and climate for their food and shelter. Because of this, their work and leisure activities often changed with the seasons.

In the spring, women farmed, using wooden spades, hoes, and digging sticks. These women farmers owned and made decisions about the land they farmed as well as the houses in which their families lived. In their fields they planted every other row with corn. Between the corn rows they planted squash and beans, whose vines would grow up the cornstalks. These three crops combine well because they grow in similar soil and climate. The Native Americans called their three major food crops— corn, squash, and beans—the three sisters.

For the Native American men, spring

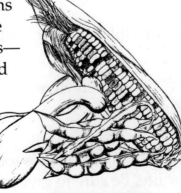

The three sisters

was a time for fishing with spears, harpoons, and nets. The women then preserved the fish by smoking them over fires made with hickory wood.

In the summer, the Haudenosaunee and the Algonquian peoples had more free time. With the crops planted, the women spent much of their time visiting friends. The men played team games. The men also had time to trade and traveled great distances to do so. A network of trade routes linked the entire North American continent. Goods moved in stages, carried by travelers from places far from New York State. The Haudenosaunee and Algonquian peoples usually had plenty of food and furs that other Native American groups wanted. This allowed the New York nations to trade for items they needed, such as flint, copper, and feathers.

When fall came, there was more work to be done. The Haudenosaunee and Algonquian nations prepared for the coming winter months, when food would be scarce. Women harvested the crops. Men hunted deer and other animals. When the hunt was over, women cooked the meat. Later they made **moccasins,** or soft leather shoes, from the skins of the deer. Men made tools and other small items from the deer antlers and bones.

After the crops were gathered, the Native Americans held harvest festivals. The purpose of these religious ceremonies was to give thanks for the plentiful food. In the winter the cold prevented farming, most hunting, and trade. Winter was

(continued)

Harcourt Brace School Publishers

a time for living indoors and resting. Children spent hours with family members listening to stories and learning the ways of their people. The men played games and talked about life in the village. Women wove baskets and created pottery for their own use or for trade.

The family was the center of Indian life. Families were **extended,** or made up of people including aunts, uncles, cousins, and grandparents. Each extended family lived close together—sometimes in one longhouse. Every family belonged to a **clan,** or a group of families who had common ancestors.

Children joined their mother's clan at birth. A man usually went to live with his wife's clan after he married. All clan members helped raise the children. Grandparents and other older family members taught the children the histories of their clans and the importance of family. Even young children took part in family life by helping with daily tasks.

Just as today, family members taught children the skills they would need as adults. Girls spent time with the women of their clan, helping them with their work. This experience taught them the skills they would need to take care of their families and contribute to their community. The men, likewise, taught boys to become good hunters and warriors.

Algonquian and Haudenosaunee children also had plenty of time to play. Girls carved dolls from wood or made them out of cornhusks. Boys competed in a variety of games and contests of skill. One of the most popular children's games was called snowsnakes. Children played it by sliding snake-shaped sticks across a frozen lake or pond.

Beaver   **Turtle**   **Wolf**   **Hawk**

Each clan had an animal symbol and was known by that animal's name.

Review

CHECK UNDERSTANDING

1. How did the Native Americans of New York use the natural resources around them?

2. What did Algonquian and Haudenosaunee children do for fun?

THINK CRITICALLY

3. Among the Native Americans of New York, women were the ones to care for farm crops. Why do you think this was so?

SHOW WHAT YOU KNOW

Imagine that you are a Native American child living in what is today New York. Write a journal entry about one day in your life. Be sure to give an animal name for your clan and for the other clans in your village.

Harcourt Brace School Publishers

Activity

Native American Culture Groups

DIRECTIONS: Read the information, and study the map below. Then answer the questions.

As glaciers formed during the last Ice Age, the amount of water in the sea went down. A thin strip of land that had been underwater was exposed above the ocean connecting Asia and North America. Some scientists believe that the first people to travel to North America may have done so by crossing this narrow strip of land, or **land bridge**. This area is now known as the Bering Strait. Slowly, over many centuries, the ancestors of the Native Americans migrated throughout North America. In time, these native people formed many different **culture groups**, or people who share a way of life. Differences in weather and geography led to differences in native cultures.

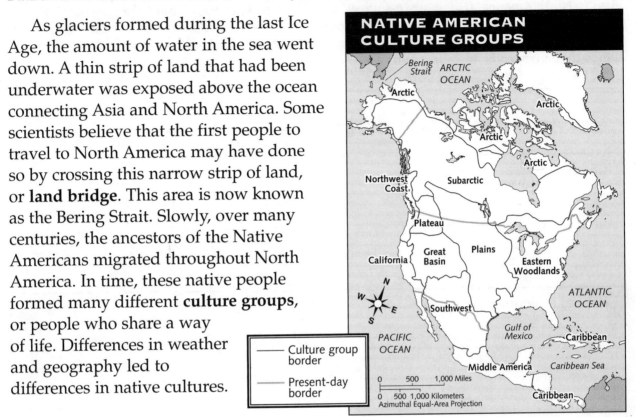

1. Which two groups occupied the largest areas in what is today the United States?

   _____

2. Which culture group were the Six Nations part of?

   _____

3. Which two groups might have been the least likely to eat fish from the ocean? Why?

   _____

4. Which group lived farthest west?

   _____

5. Locate the Bering Strait. Trace a route from the Bering Strait to New York. What were some things that might have made this journey difficult?

   _____

   _____

Harcourt Brace School Publishers

Adapting to Environments

DIRECTIONS: *Using the map on page 15, select one of the Native American culture groups that lived in North America. Use library resources and the Internet to learn about the geographical features of the area and the culture of the people you chose. Complete the chart below with information about your group. Use the last line of the chart to include customs or ways of doing things that are specific to your group.*

Name of Native American Culture Group: _____
Climate of Area
Natural Resources Available
Kinds of Food
Kinds of Housing
Special Cultural Activities

Harcourt Brace School Publishers

Native American Poems, Chants, and Stories

Native Americans created the first literature in the Americas. Most Native American poems, chants, and stories were not written down but were spoken aloud. The words were repeated from one generation to the next. As each new generation learned these poems, chants, and stories, small changes were made. For example, a word may have been added in one place or left out in another.

Many Native American poems focused on nature. Below are Native American poems from three different cultures. All three discuss some part of the natural world. The first poem, about the prairie, comes from the Chippewa (CHIH•puh•wah) people of the midwestern United States. The second poem, about the stars, is from one of the Algonquian nations in what is today New York State. The third poem is from the Yaqui (YAH•kee) people of the southwestern United States. The Yaqui poem tells of a little red quail.

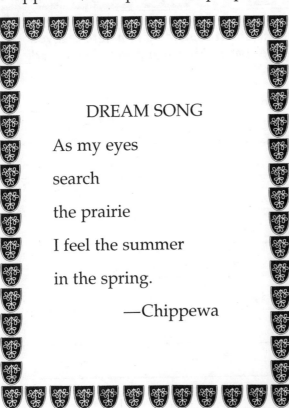

DREAM SONG

As my eyes

search

the prairie

I feel the summer

in the spring.

—Chippewa

WE ARE THE STARS
WHICH SING

We are the stars which sing,

We sing with our light;

We are the birds of fire,

We fly over the sky.

Our light is a voice;

We make a road for the spirits,

For the spirits to pass over.

Among us are three hunters

Who chase a bear.

There never was a time

When they were not hunting.

We look down on the
   mountains

This is the song of the stars.

—Algonquian

(continued)

Harcourt Brace School Publishers

LITTLE RED QUAIL

Little red quail,
    walking afar where there is no water,
        where do they make the kukupopoti sound?
Little red quail,
    walking afar where there is no water,
        where do they make the kukupopoti sound?
Over here, in the center
    of the flower-covered wilderness,
        walking afar where there is no water,
        where do they make the kukupopoti sound?
Little red quail,
    walking afar where there is no water,
        where do they make the kukupopoti sound?

—Yaqui

DIRECTIONS: After you have read the three poems, think about something in nature that you enjoy. Write a short poem about it on a separate sheet of paper. Then, copy your poem neatly on the lines provided below.

_____

_____

_____

_____

_____

_____

_____

_____

_____

Harcourt Brace School Publishers

Contributions of Native Americans

Native American influences are easily seen in today's society. New York's native Algonquian and Haudenosaunee groups contributed to the culture and development of New York State.

Many words and place names that New Yorkers use every day come from Native American languages. In fact, a number of these words come from the Algonquian and Haudenosaunee languages that were once spoken in New York State.

The English language has about 1,000 American Indian **loan words,** or words that come from other languages. Some Algonquian words still used today are *caribou, moose,* and *tomahawk.* Although the tuxedo suit is named after Tuxedo Park, New York, the word *tuxedo* comes from an Algonquian word meaning "wolf."

Many place names—for instance, the names of lakes, rivers, cities, and towns—also have their beginnings in Native American languages. In New York State, most of these place names come from the Haudenosaunee languages. *Lake Chautauqua* means "where the fish was taken out." *Genesee River* means "good valley." *Lake Ontario* means "beautiful lake." *Otsego* means "place of the rock." *Schenectady* means "on the other side of the pine lands."

Native Americans contributed to other areas of today's culture as well. Canoes, which are widely used today for fun, were invented by Native Americans and served as their main form of transportation. The Europeans traded with the Haudenosaunee people for canoes because these lightweight boats helped them travel on lakes and rivers where European ships were too large to go.

Another present-day leisure activity, the sport of lacrosse, was first played by the Haudenosaunee nations. Lacrosse fascinated the Europeans and they adopted it. The name *lacrosse* came from the French settlers who thought that the playing sticks looked like a cross on a long stick. The Native American stick design and game structure are the core of the present-day game.

Between 40,000 to 60,000 Native Americans still live in New York State today. The contributions of Native Americans to New York are much more than place names and sports. For example, the early trading routes that the Haudenosaunee people used changed from footpaths to wagon roads as Europeans moved into the area. Many of those same routes provide the basis for modern roads in use today.

Haudenosaunee lacrosse stick and ball

(continued)

Harcourt Brace School Publishers

These Native Americans have a living history. Customs and traditions from times past continue in the present. In 1794 the Haudenosaunee people signed a peace treaty with the new United States of America in Canandaigua, New York. The **treaty**, or agreement, promised "peace and friendship" between the Six Nations and the United States. As a symbol of continuing friendship, the United States promised to pay $4,500 in goods each year. The payment was to be shared equally among the clans of the Six Nations.

Today, the clan families of the Haudenosaunee Indians still receive a payment each year. The money set aside in the treaty is not paid to the Six Nations in cash, but paid in cloth. The Treaty Cloth comes to the chiefs of the Six Nations each fall. The clan mothers make sure each family gets its own piece of the cloth. Because the value of money changes over time, the amount of Treaty Cloth each family gets today is small. Yet, the Treaty Cloth of today symbolizes a peace and friendship between nations that has lasted for two centuries.

Review

CHECK UNDERSTANDING

1. What were two of the leisure activities that Native Americans contributed to our present-day society?
2. Why did Europeans want canoes?

THINK CRITICALLY

3. Why do you think it is important to understand and preserve Native American contributions?

SHOW WHAT YOU KNOW

Choose five of the following English words that have a Native American origin. Using a dictionary or reference sources, create a Native American glossary with the words you choose. Be sure to include the name of the Indian language that each word comes from and define the word as it is used today.

Native American Loan Words		
caribou	muskrat	succotash
chipmunk	opossum	tepee
hickory	pecan	terrapin
igloo	powwow	toboggan
kayak	raccoon	tomahawk
moccasin	skunk	totem
moose	squash	woodchuck

Harcourt Brace School Publishers

Activity

Wampum Belts

DIRECTIONS: Read the information about wampum below, and study the design of the Hiawatha wampum belt. Then, using graph paper, create your own wampum belt design. Mark the width of your belt on the graph paper. Next, count the number of squares needed for each pattern or shape and shade them in. Use the example below as your model.

The word *wampum* comes from the language of the Narraganset (nair•uh•GAN•suht), a nation of American Indians who lived in what is now Rhode Island. Wampum means "white shell beads." The Haudenosaunee people traded with Native Americans living on Long Island and the New England coast for beads cut out of clam shells. The Haudenosaunee people, then as now, made belts out of these purple and white beads. Wampum was traded as a form of money between Europeans and Native Americans. They used wampum because there were few metal coins in New England at that time. Strings of wampum beads were used to buy items of all kinds.

Wampum belts are mainly used as a way to remember important events. The belts' patterns and shapes **symbolize,** or stand for, different places and people involved in these events.

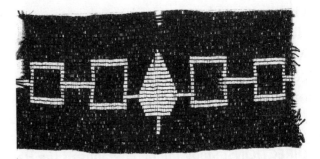

The Hiawatha wampum belt is named after the leader Hiawatha, who helped to bring the Haudenosaunee people together.

The Hiawatha belt is perhaps the most famous and important wampum belt used for this purpose. Its design describes the formation of the Five Nations. A pine tree in the center represents the Onondaga. The four rectangles all around the tree stand for the other member nations, the Mohawk, Oneida, Cayuga, and Seneca. Another famous wampum belt showing Huron Indian warriors with their shields was presented to a French official as a symbol of Huron strength.

Harcourt Brace School Publishers

Example of a wampum belt design on graph paper

Haudenosaunee Combs

The handcrafted combs shown on this page were made by Onondaga and Seneca carvers. These combs were both useful and attractive. Women, children, and men wore combs to decorate their hair and hold it in place. Making combs was a skilled craft. A comb-maker would carve the comb out of wood, bone, or the antler of a deer or moose, using a sharp stone.

The Onondaga comb was made in this way.

By the late 1500s the Haudenosaunee people were trading with Europeans for metal tools. The metal tools were sharper and smaller so carvers could make combs with more teeth and more difficult designs. The Seneca comb is an example made with the new tools.

DIRECTIONS: *Study the photographs of the Haudenosaunee combs. Then use the graphic organizer below to compare and contrast the two combs.*

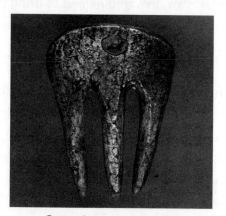

Onondaga comb, 1550

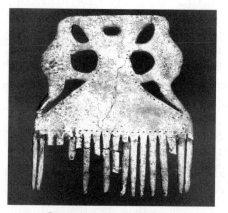

Seneca comb, 1678

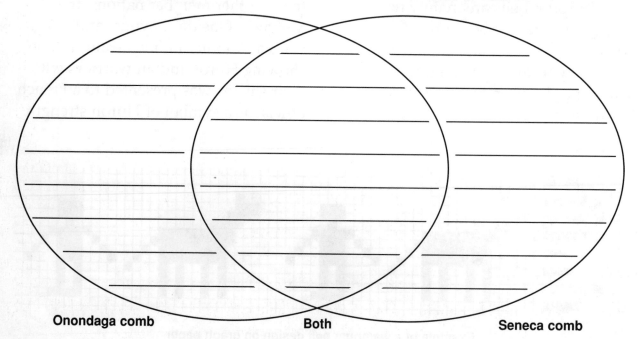

Onondaga comb   **Both**   **Seneca comb**

Harcourt Brace School Publishers

Your Community

Native American Heritage

DIRECTIONS: Use the library or the Internet to help you find out more about the early Native Americans who lived long ago in your community. Then follow the steps below to help you complete the chart.

- Using a map of New York State and your community, find and list at least five place names that come from Algonquian or Haudenosaunee (Iroquois) words. Suitable place names include the names of lakes, rivers, communities, and streets.

- Find out which Native American language the names came from and what they mean. Write this information in the table as well.

Place Name	Language	Meaning
1.		
2.		
3.		
4.		
5.		

Harcourt Brace School Publishers

Unit 1 Practice Test

PART I: MULTIPLE-CHOICE

DIRECTIONS: (Questions 1–10) Choose the best answer for each question or incomplete statement. Circle the letter of the answer you choose.

1. During the Woodland period, Native Americans in New York State first began to

   A hunt animals.

   C live in villages.

   B cut down trees.

   D gather nuts and berries.

2. Which of the following Native American nations belonged to the Algonquian group?

   A Mahican

   C Seneca

   B Oneida

   D Onondaga

3. The members of the Haudenosaunee joined together mainly to

   A trade with other nations.

   C learn the ways of the Europeans.

   B protect themselves.

   D adopt a single language.

4. Which of these was an important crop for Native Americans in New York State?

   A tomatoes

   C cotton

   B corn

   D beets

5. Among the Haudenosaunee and the Algonquian nations, which of these jobs was generally done by women?

   A hunting

   C fishing

   B making tools

   D farming

6. A group of Native American families with a common ancestor is called a

   A tribe.

   C wigwam.

   B nation.

   D clan.

7. Which one of the following is a Native American contribution to today's culture?

   A baseball

   C canoes

   B religion

   D farming

Harcourt Brace School Publishers

8. Which of the following words is a Native American loan word in English?

A moccasin

B bluebird

C river

D flower

Use the map below to answer Questions 9 and 10.

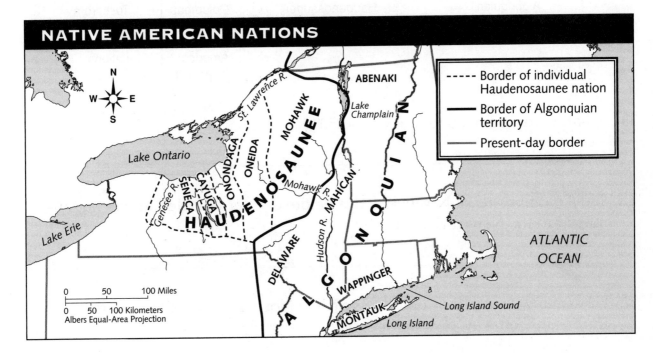

9. Which one of the following nations belonged to the Algonquian group?

A Seneca

B Onondaga

C Cayuga

D Delaware

10. Three of the Haudenosaunee nations lived alongside which body of water?

A Long Island Sound

B Atlantic Ocean

C Lake Ontario

D Lake Champlain

Harcourt Brace School Publishers

PART II: CONSTRUCTED RESPONSE ITEMS

DIRECTIONS: (Questions 11–20) Write your answer to each question on the lines provided.

Use the time line below to answer questions 11–13.

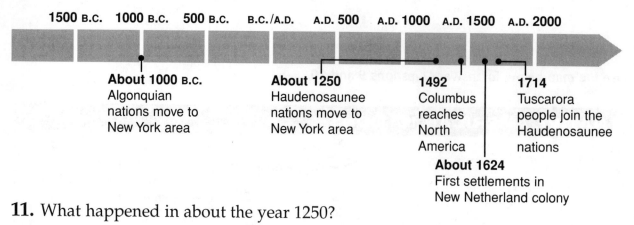

1500 B.C.   1000 B.C.   500 B.C.   B.C./A.D.   A.D. 500   A.D. 1000   A.D. 1500   A.D. 2000

About 1000 B.C.
Algonquian
nations move to
New York area

About 1250
Haudenosaunee
nations move to
New York area

1492
Columbus
reaches
North
America

1714
Tuscarora
people join the
Haudenosaunee
nations

About 1624
First settlements in
New Netherland colony

11. What happened in about the year 1250?

_____

12. Did Columbus reach North America before or after the Algonquian nations moved to the New York area?

_____

13. How many years after Columbus reached North America did the first Europeans settle in New Netherland?

_____

For Questions 14-15, look at the pictures. Then answer the questions below.

Picture A   **Picture B**

14. What are the names of these two kinds of Native American shelters?

Picture A: _____   Picture B: _____

15. What natural resources do these shelters use?

_____

Harcourt Brace School Publishers

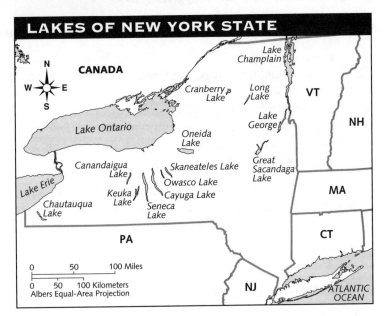

LAKES OF NEW YORK STATE

16. Which lake forms part of the border between New York and Vermont?

_____

17. Which three lakes were named after Haudenosaunee nations?

_____

18. More Native American settlements were located in the central and western parts of New York State. Why do you think that was so?

_____

Look at this picture of the Hiawatha wampum belt to help you answer Questions 19 and 20.

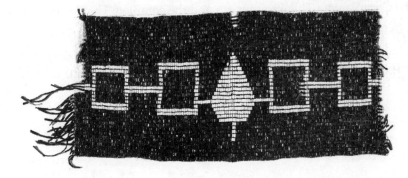

19. What natural resources do wampum belts use?

_____

20. What does the design on the Hiawatha wampum belt stand for?

_____

Harcourt Brace School Publishers

PART III: DOCUMENT-BASED QUESTIONS

DIRECTIONS: *This part of the practice test is designed to find out how well you think and write in social studies.*

Historical Background: The Haudenosaunee (Iroquois) nations, or the Five Nations, lived by certain rules and traditions. These rules and traditions were guidelines for their way of life. They reflect Haudenosaunee beliefs about community, family, and nature.

Below are some documents related to the Haudenosaunee nations. The first is the *Iroquois Constitution,* a written statement of Haudenosaunee oral history. The second is part of a student's research project. The third is a textbook feature.

Task: Write an essay about how the Haudenosaunee nations lived. In your essay, tell what was most important to the Haudenosaunee people, and describe rules they followed. Use the documents below and the answers you give in Part A to help you write your essay.

PART A: SHORT ANSWER

Look at each document, and answer the questions that follow.

Document 1 From the Iroquois Constitution

44. The [families] of the people of the Five Nations shall run in the female line. Women shall own the land and the soil. Men and women shall follow the status of the mother.

45. The women heirs of the Confederated Lordship titles shall be called Royaneh (Noble) for all time to come.

50. The Royaneh women of the Confederacy heirs of the Lordship titles shall elect two women of their family as cooks for the Lord when the people shall assemble at his house for business or other purposes.

It is not good nor honorable for a Confederate Lord to allow his people whom he has called to go hungry.

53. When the Royaneh women, holders of a Lordship title, select one of their sons as a candidate, they shall select one who is trustworthy, of good character, of honest disposition, one who manages his own affairs, supports his own family, if any, and who has proven a faithful man to his Nation.

101. It shall be the duty of the appointed managers of the Thanksgiving festivals to do all that is needed for carrying out the duties of the occasions.

The recognized festivals of Thanksgiving shall be the Midwinter Thanksgiving, the Maple or Sugar-making Thanksgiving . . . the Cornplanting Thanksgiving . . . and the complete Thanksgiving of the Harvest.

Each nation's festivals shall be held in their Long Houses.

What are three examples of rules set up by the Iroquois Constitution?

_____

_____

_____

Harcourt Brace School Publishers

Document 2 Haudenosaunee: Culture & History

From Student Research Notes

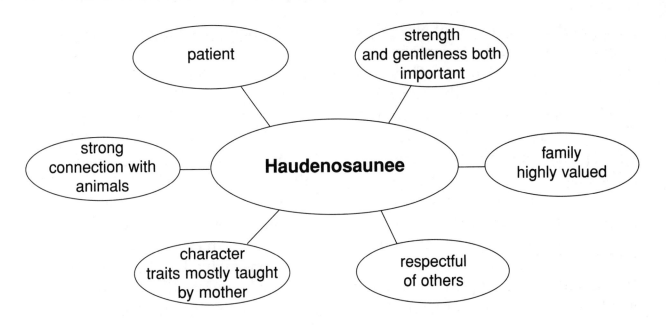

What does this web suggest about Haudenosaunee beliefs?

_____

_____

Document 3 Textbook Feature

Corn

The three most important crops to the Haudenosaunee (Iroquois) were corn, beans, and squash. These crops were so important that they were called the Three Sisters in their religion. The most celebrated of these crops was corn. The Iroquois held three different festivals related to either the growing or the harvesting of corn. These festivals were the Corn-Planting Festival, the Green-Corn Festival, and the Corn-Gathering Festival.

How has corn been important to the way of life of the Haudenosaunee people?

_____

_____

PART B: ESSAY RESPONSE

On a separate sheet of paper, write an essay about how the Haudenosaunee nations lived. Use the documents and the answers you gave in Part A to help you plan your essay.

In your essay, remember to:
- Identify some of the rules the Haudenosaunee people followed
- Explain some of the beliefs of the Haudenosaunee people
- Describe the importance of corn to the Haudenosaunee way of life

Harcourt Brace School Publishers

Early Europeans in North America

The Native Americans of New York were well aware of the geography of their part of North America. They knew of the great sea to the east, over which the sun rose. Today we know that sea as the Atlantic Ocean. The native people of New York did not know that another continent lay across this huge ocean. They also never imagined that some day huge ships would come from far across the sea and change their way of life forever.

The people of Europe did not know about the Native Americans, either. In fact, Europeans were unaware that the continents of North America and South America even existed. They first came to this continent by mistake. The European explorers were really trying to find a faster way to reach Asia.

Europeans had been trading with the people of Asia for hundreds of years. They bought spices, such as pepper, cinnamon, and cloves, from the people of Asia. They also traded European crops and products for Asian silks, jewels, and fine pottery. Communities that trade with one another for products that they cannot make are **interdependent.**

Europeans called the Asian lands the *Indies.* Most Europeans traveled to the Indies by land. They went from Europe into Asia on a route known as the Silk Road. Some people began to think that a sea route around the tip of Africa would be the easiest way to get from Europe to the Indies. A few people thought sailing west across the Atlantic Ocean might get them to the Indies even faster. One of these people was Christopher Columbus.

In 1492 Columbus and his crew sailed from Europe across the Atlantic Ocean. They believed that if they sailed far enough west, they would circle the Earth and reach the Indies. Columbus never made it to the Indies—the Americas got in his way! Columbus arrived at the islands that are now known as the Bahamas. Because he thought he had reached the Indies, he called the native people he met there *Indians.* This is why we sometimes refer to the first people to live in North America as American Indians.

The astrolabe, an invention once used by sailors to find their way at sea

(continued)

Harcourt Brace School Publishers

Soon after Columbus's voyage, many Europeans realized that North America and South America were not part of the Indies. They understood that they were continents that had never been explored. Some European people started to call these continents the "New World."

Still looking for a sea route to Asia, European explorers began to search for a way to sail around or through North America. They called this hoped-for sea route the **Northwest Passage.** The search for the Northwest Passage is what brought European explorers to the land now known as New York State.

The first European to set foot in New York was Giovanni da Verrazano (joh•VAH•nee dah veh•ruht•SAH•noh). Verrazano was from Italy, but he grew up in France. The French government hired Verrazano to find the Northwest Passage. In 1524 he sailed west

from Europe. Traveling along North America's coast, he sailed into what is now known as New York Harbor. There he saw the land where New York City would someday stand. He wrote of the site, "It is not without some . . . value." Verrazano did not find the Northwest Passage so he left the Americas and returned to Europe.

Verrazano's visit to what would become New York State was short. Yet, it was the beginning of something important. Within the next 100 years, Europeans would begin to come across the sea in larger numbers. The Americas would never be the same.

Review

CHECK UNDERSTANDING

1. Where was Columbus trying to go when he reached North America?
2. What was Verrazano looking for when he came to New York?

THINK CRITICALLY

3. Look at a globe or a map of the world. Why do you think the Europeans first sailed east to reach Asia rather than west?

SHOW WHAT YOU KNOW

Imagine that you are a European explorer. You have just been hired to sail across the Atlantic Ocean to find a faster sea route to the Indies. You need a crew to help you on your journey. Design a poster that advertises your trip. Be sure it explains why people should join you.

Harcourt Brace School Publishers

Activity

European Explorers in New York

DIRECTIONS: Read the paragraphs and study the map on page 33. Then answer the questions that follow.

Nearly 100 years passed between Verrazano's visit and the next European explorer's landing in New York. This explorer was an Englishman named Henry Hudson.

Hudson had been hired by the Dutch to search for the Northwest Passage through the Americas. The Dutch are people from the Netherlands, a country also known as Holland. At that time the

Henry Hudson

Netherlands was a rich trading nation in Europe. Business people in the Netherlands formed large companies to trade with other Europeans. The most important of these trading companies was the Dutch East India Company.

The Dutch East India Company was eager to find the Northwest Passage. Hudson was given a ship called the *Half Moon* and about 20 sailors. With his ship and crew, Hudson headed across the Atlantic Ocean.

In 1609 Hudson sailed into what is today New York Harbor. He landed near where Verrazano had 85 years earlier. As Hudson explored the area, he noticed a large river flowing into the harbor. Hudson decided to sail

north up the river. Later, this river would be named the Hudson River in his honor. Hudson continued to sail north to what is today Albany. He soon realized that the river would not lead to the Indies. Disappointed, he turned back.

Around the same time, a French explorer named Samuel de Champlain (sham•PLAYN) made several trips across the Atlantic Ocean. He explored the areas now known as southern Canada and northern New York State.

While exploring, Champlain and his crew met some Native Americans and established good relations with them. In 1609 Champlain and two members of his crew joined forces with the Algonquian peoples and the Huron nation. Together they attacked the Haudenosaunee nations living in New York. In the course of the fighting, Champlain became the first European to explore much of the land and bodies of water

Samuel de Champlain

in what is now northern New York State. He even named one of the lakes he found after himself.

(continued)

Harcourt Brace School Publishers

Despite Hudson's and Champlain's explorations of New York, much of the area was still unknown to Europeans. Yet, thanks to these explorers, two important things became clear. The land that would someday be known as New York State had many natural resources. It was also home to many groups of Native Americans.

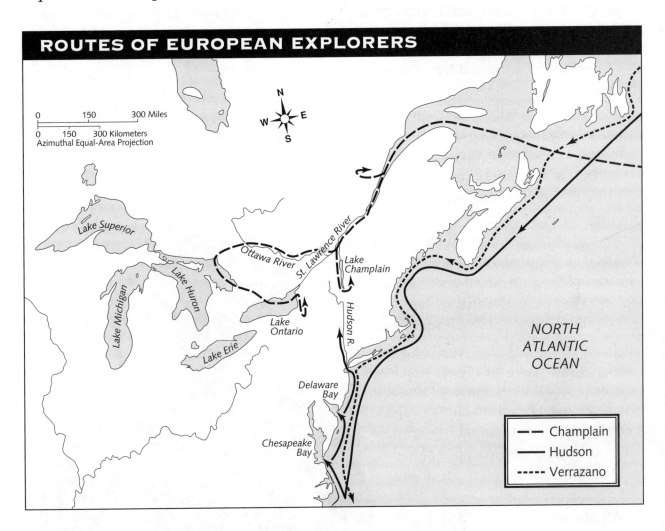

ROUTES OF EUROPEAN EXPLORERS

1. What three explorers' routes are shown on the map?

   _____

2. What two bays did Hudson explore?

   _____

3. On which two Great Lakes did Champlain explore?

   _____

4. How do you think historians know the sea routes the explorers took?

   _____

   _____

Harcourt Brace School Publishers

An Explorer Writes About New York

Many European explorers kept journals that described their adventures. Below is an entry from the journal kept by Giovanni da Verrazano as he explored areas of New York.

"After having remained here three days, riding at anchor on the coast, as we could find no harbor we determined to . . . coast along the shore to the north-east, keeping sail on the vessel only by day, and coming to anchor by night. After proceeding one hundred leagues [300 miles], we found a very pleasant situation among some steep hills, through which a very large river, deep at its mouth, forced its way to the sea. . . .

. . . But as we were riding at anchor in a good berth [safe distance] we would not venture up in our vessel, without a knowledge of the mouth; therefore we took the [small] boat, and entering the river, we found the country on its banks well peopled, the inhabitants . . . being dressed out with the feathers of birds of various colors. They came towards us with . . . delight, raising loud shouts of admiration, and showing us where we could most securely land with our boat. We passed up this river, about half a league [1 1/2 miles], when we found it formed a most beautiful lake . . . upon which they were rowing thirty or more of their small boats, from one shore to the other, filled with multitudes who came to see us.

All of a sudden, as is [likely] to happen to navigators, a violent contrary wind blew in from the sea, and forced us to return to our ship, greatly regretting to leave this region which seemed so [big] and delightful, and which we supposed must also contain great riches, as the hills showed many indications of minerals."

Terra-cotta sculpture of Italian explorer Giovanni da Verrazano, made around the 1520s

Harcourt Brace School Publishers

(continued)

DIRECTIONS: Reread Verrazano's story. Pay close attention to the descriptions of the land and the people. On a separate sheet of paper, write a story from the point of view of the Native Americans seeing Verrazano's ship and European people for the first time. Use the chart below to help you plan your story.

Title	
Setting	
Main Characters	
Plot Details	

Harcourt Brace School Publishers

Native Americans and Europeans Meet

The first meeting between European explorers and the native people living in what is now New York State went well. The Native Americans seemed happy to meet the Europeans. Not all meetings between Native Americans and Europeans went as well. When Henry Hudson sailed north he and his crew fought with some Mohawks living on the shores.

Samuel de Champlain was not warmly welcomed by all the native people he met, either. At one point he found himself in the middle of a battle between Native American nations.

Why did Native Americans and Europeans fight at some times and not at others? Some nations welcomed the Europeans because they saw them as possible **allies,** or friends, who would help them in a war against other Indian nations. The Native Americans also wanted to **trade,** or exchange goods, with Europeans. Many of the goods the Europeans offered could not be found elsewhere. Some of these goods included European knives, metal tools and cooking pots, as well as certain kinds of beads and clothing.

Other Native Americans did not want to be friendly with the Europeans. They saw Europeans as outsiders who were coming to take their land and use up its natural resources. They became frightened by the power of some European inventions, such as guns.

Over time, more and more Europeans **migrated,** or moved, into North America. Native Americans realized that these people were not just visitors. Many Native Americans learned to live peacefully with the new settlers. Others fought to try to turn them away.

Review

CHECK UNDERSTANDING

1. What were two reasons some Native Americans welcomed Europeans?
2. What were two reasons some Native Americans did not welcome Europeans?

THINK CRITICALLY

3. Why do you think Native Americans wanted European goods?

SHOW WHAT YOU KNOW

Imagine that you are the leader of a Native American village. Many Europeans have settled in your area. Should your village become friends with the Europeans? Write a speech about your decision. Be sure to include reasons for your decision.

Harcourt Brace School Publishers

Activity

Two Worlds Come Together

DIRECTIONS: Read the paragraphs. Then illustrate the Columbian Exchange on the map below. First, draw two arrows to show how plants moved between Europe and North America. Then, draw two more arrows to show how animals moved between the two continents. Next, label the arrows with the names of plants and animals that were exchanged in each direction.

Soon after Native Americans and Europeans met, they began to trade goods. This exchange of goods, plants, animals, and ideas between the Americas and Europe is now known as the **Columbian Exchange**. It was named after Christopher Columbus.

Explorers returned to Europe from the Americas with many new plants, such as corn, peanuts, potatoes, sweet potatoes, and tomatoes. In turn, explorers introduced plants such as wheat, barley, peas, and sugarcane into the Americas. At the same time, they brought many European ideas, manners, and clothing. Although they did not intend it, diseases like smallpox followed.

Animals were also a large part of the Columbian Exchange. The Europeans brought over animals such as cats, horses, pigs, sheep, cattle, chickens, goats, and honeybees. They took back American wild animals such as gray squirrels, guinea pigs, muskrats, and turkeys.

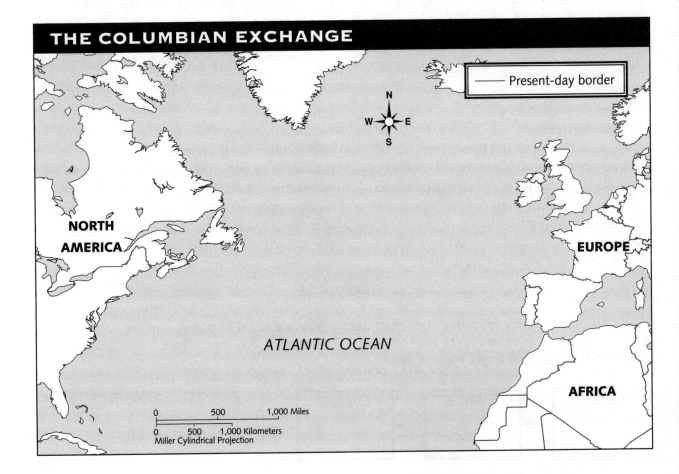

THE COLUMBIAN EXCHANGE

—— Present-day border

N
W   E
S

NORTH AMERICA

EUROPE

ATLANTIC OCEAN

AFRICA

0   500   1,000 Miles
0   500   1,000 Kilometers
Miller Cylindrical Projection

Harcourt Brace School Publishers

Native Americans Meet Hudson

Most of what is known about the first meetings between Europeans and Native Americans comes from European writings. The Native Americans of New York did not have written languages at that time. They remembered events by repeating the information from one generation to the next and by creating wampum belts. In the 1700s a European named John Heckewelder met with many Native Americans and wrote down their stories. One of these stories told of the first meeting between Henry Hudson and the native peoples of New York. Part of this story is written below.

"A great many years ago, when men with a white skin had never yet been seen in this land, some Indians who were . . . fishing, at a place where the sea widens, saw at a great distance something remarkably large floating on the water, and such as they had never seen before. . . . but they could not agree upon what it was; some believed it to be an uncommonly large fish or animal, while others believed it must be a very big house floating on the sea. . . . They saw this wonderful object was moving towards the land, and that it must be an animal or something else that had life in it; it would therefore be proper to inform all the Indians . . . of what they had seen, and put them on their guard. . . .

These Indians arriving in numbers . . . and observing that it was actually moving towards the entrance of the river or bay; concluded it to be a remarkably large house in which the Mannitto (the Great or Supreme Being) himself was present, and that he probably was coming to visit them. . . .

[B]ut other runners soon after arriving declare that it is positively a house full of human beings, of quite a different color from that of the Indians, and dressed differently from them; that in particular one of them was dressed entirely in red. . . . They are called to from the vessel in a language they do not understand, yet they shout or yell in return by way of answer; . . . many are for running off to the woods, but are pressed by others to stay . . .

The house . . . at last stops, and a canoe of a smaller size comes on shore with the red man, and some others in it; some stay with his canoe to guard it. The chiefs and wise men, assembled in council, form themselves into a large circle, towards which the man in red clothes approaches with two others. He salutes them with a friendly face, and they return the salute. . . . They are lost in admiration; the dress, the manners, the whole appearance of the unknown strangers is to them a subject of wonder; but they are particularly struck with him who wore the red coat all glittering with gold lace, which they could in no manner account for."

DIRECTIONS: *Copy the following flow chart onto a separate sheet of paper. Use the flow chart to record four major events in the order that they happened in the story. Then, in the last box, predict what you think might happen next.*

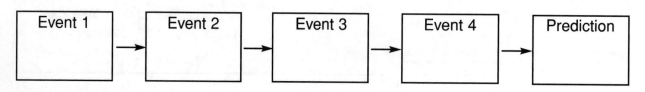

| Event 1 | | Event 2 | | Event 3 | | Event 4 | | Prediction |

Harcourt Brace School Publishers

The Dutch in New York

In 1609 the Dutch government sent Henry Hudson to explore the area that would become New York State. Hudson claimed lands along the Hudson River for the Netherlands. The Dutch called the land New Netherland.

The first Dutch people in the New Netherland colony arrived in the Hudson River valley. A **colony** is a settlement separated from, but under the control of, a home country. Dutch people came to New Netherland to trade with the Native Americans for furs—especially beaver furs. The traders shipped these furs back to Europe where they were sold for a high price. The settlements built by these trappers and traders were not really villages but just small trading posts.

In 1621 a new trading company called the Dutch West India Company formed. The owners of the new Dutch West India Company decided to use the colony of New Netherland as a base for trade. To create this base, they needed to build permanent settlements in the colony. In 1624 the company paid for about 30 Dutch families to sail to New Netherland and live there permanently.

These first settlers, or **colonists**, built Fort Orange. This fort was on the site of present-day Albany. Fort Orange was the first permanent European settlement in New Netherland. It was located on the Hudson River. Fort Orange was farther inland than any other European colony at that time.

The next year another group of settlers sent by the Dutch West India Company started a town on Manhattan Island. Manhattan is the long, narrow island at the mouth of the Hudson River in New York Harbor. The island gets its name from the Indian word *Man-a-hat-a*. The Dutch settlement was made up of a fort and a few houses. At first, the Dutch called the settlement Fort Amsterdam. When it grew beyond its use as a fort, it was renamed New Amsterdam.

The town of New Amsterdam continued to grow and soon needed a leader. The settlers chose Peter Minuit (MIN•yuh•wuht) to lead the town. In 1626 he bought Manhattan from the local Native Americans. In this famous trade he gave the Native Americans two boxes filled with goods such as kettles, cloth, and beads in exchange for all of

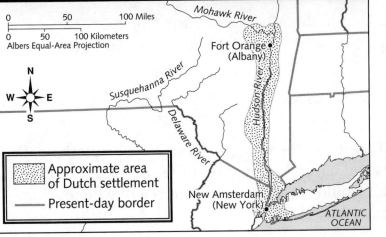

DUTCH SETTLEMENT IN NEW YORK

(continued)

Harcourt Brace School Publishers

Manhattan Island. The value of the goods was about $24. Today that amount equals several thousand United States dollars. It was a very small amount to pay for such a large piece of land.

By 1630 the Dutch had started several more small trading posts and settlements in the colony. Still, the European population remained no more than 1,000 people. The Dutch government decided to encourage settlement of the colony through a reward system. Under this system **patroons,** or owners of large pieces of land, could bring up to 50 adults each from Europe to settle their land in the new colony of New Netherland.

The landowners were each given 18 miles, (29 km) worth of land that faced onto the Hudson River. They were told

t' Fort nieuw Amsterdam op de Manhatans

New Amsterdam, 1626

that they could expand inland as far as they wished. They also received fishing and hunting rights, animals, tools, and housing. In return, settlers on the land paid the patroons rent and gave them extra crops.

The population of the colony of New Netherland would not stay small for long. The Dutch were not the only people who wanted to settle there.

Review

CHECK UNDERSTANDING

1. What explorer first claimed land in the Americas for the Dutch?
2. What was the first Dutch settlement in New York? Where was it located?

THINK CRITICALLY

3. Both of the first Dutch settlements included forts. Why do you think this was so?

SHOW WHAT YOU KNOW

Design a flyer inviting people to settle in the new colony of New Netherland. Be sure to describe the settlements and natural resources of the area. Also, include any other information you think would make people want to move there. Then illustrate your flyer with a map or drawing.

Harcourt Brace School Publishers

Life in New Netherland

DIRECTIONS: Read the paragraphs below. As you read, look for the main idea within each paragraph. Then, underline the sentence that tells the main idea. Remember, the main idea sentence may or may not be at the beginning of the paragraph.

At first, New Netherland colonists feared Native American attacks so they built forts for protection. The settlement at Fort Orange had strong walls to protect the settlers. The settlers lived in houses inside the fort. They also dug a ditch called a moat around the outside of the fort. The settlers could leave the fort to care for their crops and graze their livestock in pastures. Although they used the Hudson River mainly for transportation, it also provided protection on one side.

Because the Dutch could not find a crop that grew well in the soil of New Netherland, they depended on trade with Native Americans. The Dutch settlers and Native Americans formed a partnership. The Native Americans depended on the Dutch settlers as allies against their enemies. Most Indian nations only traded and allied with one European country.

How did the Dutch people act toward the Native Americans? The Dutch treated Native Americans better than most other Europeans did. The Dutch did not mind that the Native American ways of life and religious beliefs differed from theirs. Most differences between Dutch colonists and Native Americans were over land or trade. The Dutch believed in "live and let live," as long as nothing stopped trade.

At first, the government ruling New Netherland was disorganized. Native Americans and other European settlers often did not recognize Dutch claims to land. The competition for hunting grounds to supply the fur trade often led to war between Native American nations. Hunting for furs also began to lower the number of animals in the area. As you can see, the Dutch focus on business led to some problems in the New Netherland colony.

Peter Stuyvesant (STY•vuh•suhnt) made many changes when he became governor of the New Netherland colony in 1647. Soon after his arrival he began to work to turn New Netherland into a more orderly colony. Until that time, it had been little more than a number of loosely connected trading posts. Under Stuyvesant the colony made peace with unfriendly Indian nations and other European colonies. The colony also began to farm more. This meant that the fur trade was no longer the only way for settlers to live.

The Dutch colony of New Netherland existed for only about 60 years, but some Dutch influences can still be seen today. Many of the Christmas traditions, including Santa Claus, were brought to the United States by Dutch colonists. Children left their wooden shoes by the fireplace to be filled with gifts by Santa Claus. The Dutch influenced New York place names as well. The cities of Brooklyn and Rensselaer still have names given to them by Dutch settlers.

Fort Orange

Harcourt Brace School Publishers

Slave Ships

DIRECTIONS: Read the paragraphs below. Then study the diagram of the slave ship. Use this information to complete the activities on page 43.

Around the same time that the Dutch settled the New Netherland colony, the English began to form their own colonies on the east coast of North America. From the start there were not enough people to do all the work of setting up colonies. Clearing land of trees and rocks so that it could be farmed was difficult. Having enough people to work in the fields of large farms was also a problem.

The Dutch, English, and other Europeans decided to solve the problem of not enough workers by using slaves. **Slaves** are people who are held against their will and forced to work for no pay. From the beginning there were people who felt that slavery was wrong, but the colonial governments allowed it.

Both the Dutch and the English often used slaves to do their hardest work. Slaves were thought of as property and were often treated poorly. They could be beaten or punished in other ways when they did not do as the slave owners told them. If they tried to run away, they were often caught and returned. Some slaves were killed for trying to escape.

The slaves were people from the continent of Africa. These people had been captured and brought across the Atlantic Ocean to the Americas by men known as slave traders. Trading in slaves was a money-making business. European trading companies, such as the Dutch West Indies Company, made deals with African governments. The African governments would then capture and sell neighboring or enemy people.

Many people died in their struggle to stay free. Many others died on the trip to the Americas. Slaves were packed into slave ships and chained together below the decks. There was little food or water. The ships were

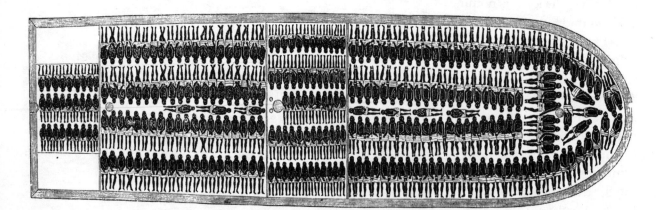

Diagram of the inside of a slave ship

(continued)

Harcourt Brace School Publishers

filthy, causing the spread of disease and many deaths. It is thought that as many as half the captured slaves died before reaching the Americas.

Children born to slave parents were also slaves. Often families were torn apart. Parents were separated from their children and husbands from their wives by being sold. Slaves had no **rights**, or freedoms, not even the right to keep their families together.

A few slave owners allowed slaves to earn their own freedom. Some owners freed their slaves as a reward for faithful service. However, most of the time slavery lasted a person's entire lifetime.

Slaves in colonial New York rebelled against the slave system in the 1700s. Since they lived in cities they were able to band together and try to fight for freedom. Many people, including free European colonists that tried to help them, were hanged for this act of rebellion.

Slavery became an important question when the United States was formed. It was a question that was not settled until Americans fought a war over it.

1. About how many people would you guess were packed into the slave ship?

_____

2. Why do you think slave traders crowded so many people together?

_____

_____

_____

3. How does the picture on page 42 show that slave ships were unpleasant places?

_____

_____

_____

4. What words would you use to describe the picture?

_____

_____

_____

_____

Harcourt Brace School Publishers

Your Community

Natural Resources

One of the things that most attracted European settlers to the area now known as New York State was its natural resources. Some of New York State's natural resources are its trees, land, plants, animals, rivers, lakes, and minerals.

DIRECTIONS: Visit the library or use the Internet to learn about the natural resources in your community. On the table below, write the information you find. Then choose the natural resource that you think is most important in your community. Explain why it is so important.

Natural Resources in My Community		
Name of Natural Resource	**Where It Is Located**	**What People Use It For**
1.		
2.		
3.		

_____ is the most important natural resource in my

community because _____

_____

_____

_____

_____

_____

_____

Harcourt Brace School Publishers

Unit 2 Practice Test

PART I: MULTIPLE-CHOICE

DIRECTIONS: (Questions 1–10) Choose the best answer to each question or incomplete statement. Circle the letter of the answer you choose.

1. The main goal of the first Europeans who explored North America was to

   A trade with Native Americans.

   C buy land.

   B find a faster route to Asia.

   D start settlements in New York.

2. Who was the first European to arrive in what is today New York State?

   A Samuel de Champlain

   C Henry Hudson

   B Christopher Columbus

   D Giovanni da Verrazano

3. What were both Verrazano and Hudson trying to find?

   A the Northwest Passage

   C a safe harbor for large ships

   B trading partners

   D Native American villages

4. Samuel de Champlain was the first European to

   A see the Atlantic Ocean.

   C explore what is now northern New York State.

   B sail the Hudson River.

   D arrive at New York Harbor.

5. Which sentence best describes the Haudenosaunee people's first experience with Champlain?

   A They established a fur trade with Champlain.

   C They fought against Champlain and other Native Americans.

   B They began to work for Champlain.

   D They welcomed him into their lands.

6. The first European settlers in what is now New York State were

   A English.

   C French.

   B Dutch.

   D Italian.

Harcourt Brace School Publishers

7. When the first Europeans settled the land now known as New York, they named it

A New Netherland.

B Albany.

C the Dutch East Indies.

D Canada.

8. Peter Minuit is known as the person who

A discovered New York Harbor.

B founded Fort Orange.

C explored the Hudson River.

D bought Manhattan Island.

Use the map below to answer Questions 9 and 10.

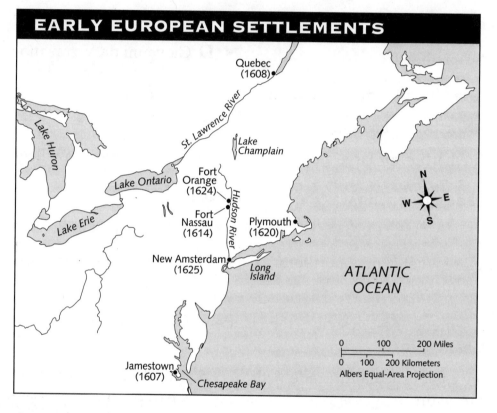

9. Which settlement was founded in 1625?

A Plymouth

B Fort Orange

C Quebec

D New Amsterdam

10. Fort Orange was located on which body of water?

A New York Harbor

B St. Lawrence River

C Hudson River

D Lake Champlain

Harcourt Brace School Publishers

PART II: CONSTRUCTED RESPONSE ITEMS

DIRECTIONS: (Questions 11–20) Write your answer to each question on the lines provided.
Use the map below to answer Questions 11–13.

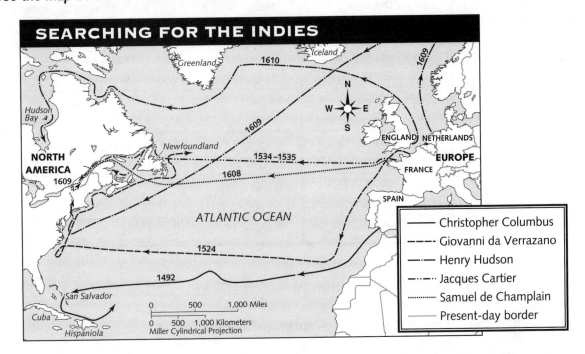

11. According to the map, who were the first two explorers to sail west in search

of the Indies? _____

12. What area did Henry Hudson explore in 1610? _____

13. Which explorer did not go to the North American mainland?

_____

For Questions 14–15, complete the table below. Write at least two examples in each empty box.

THE COLUMBIAN EXCHANGE		
Contribution	From North America to Europe	From Europe to North America
14. Plants		wheat barley peas sugar
15. Animals	squirrels guinea pigs muskrats turkeys	

Harcourt Brace School Publishers

Use the table below to answer Questions 16–17.

EUROPEAN EXPLORERS			
Name	**Date**	**Nation Sailed For**	**What He Explored**
Christopher Columbus	1492	Spain	Bahamas
Giovanni Caboto	1497	England	Newfoundland, Canada
Giovanni da Verrazano	1524	France	Atlantic coast, New York Harbor
Samuel de Champlain	1608	France	Parts of Canada and northern New York
Henry Hudson	1609	Netherlands	New York Harbor, Hudson River
	1610	England	Hudson Bay

16. Which explorer sailed for two different nations? _____

17. Which explorers traveled in what is now New York State? _____

For Questions 18–20, read the paragraphs below.

In 1625 three ships sailed from the Netherlands. They were bound for the Dutch colony in North America. The names of the ships were the Horse, the Sheep, and the Cow. A number of Dutch settlers sailed on board, but the ships mainly held animals for the new farms the settlers hoped to build in the New Netherland colony.

By 1630 nearly 1,000 Dutch settlers lived in the Hudson River valley, from New Amsterdam to Fort Orange. Since Henry Hudson had explored this area, the Dutch lay claim to this land. The first settlements in this colony were built as forts to protect colonists from a Native American attack.

18. What were the three ships from the Netherlands carrying?

_____

19. Where were the ships going, and why?

_____

20. Why were some of the first Dutch settlements in New York built as forts?

_____

Harcourt Brace School Publishers

PART III: DOCUMENT-BASED QUESTIONS

DIRECTIONS: This part of the practice test is designed to find out how well you think and write in social studies.

Historical Background: When Europeans reached North America, they met many Native Americans. Both Europeans and Native Americans were unsure of what to expect from each other. These two groups both looked for ways they could relate to one another.

Below are documents that tell how the two groups of people felt and acted toward each other. The first is a journal of a European explorer. The second describes the Native American view of Europeans. The third document reports the progress of the Europeans in their effort to settle a North American colony.

Task: Write an essay about Native American and European reactions to each other. In your essay, describe how European and Native American views of each other were different and how they were similar. Use the documents below and the answers you give in Part A to help you write your essay.

PART A: SHORT ANSWER

Look at each document, and answer the questions that follow.

Document 1

From the journals of Robert Juet, who sailed with Henry Hudson on his trip on the Hudson River

Sept. 12, 1609 "This morning at our first [split] in the river, there came eight and twenty canoes full of men, women and children to betray us. But we saw their intent, and suffered none of them to come aboard. . . . They brought with them oysters and beans, [and we] bought some. They have great tobacco pipes of yellow copper, and pots of earth to [cook] their meats in."

Sept. 15, 1609 "This morning our two savages got out of a [window] and swam away. After we were under sail, they called to us in scorn. At night we came to the other mountains, which lie from the rivers side. There we found very loving people, and very old men. . . . Our boat went to fish, and caught [many] very good fish."

Sept. 16, 1609 "In the morning our boat went again to fishing, but [we caught] few, [because] their canoes had been there all night. This morning the people came aboard, and brought us ears of Indian corn, and pumpkins, and tobacco: which we bought for trifles."

Sept. 19, 1609 "The people of the country came flocking aboard and brought us grapes, and pumpkins, which we bought for trifles. And many brought us beaver skins, and otter skins, which we bought for beads, knives, and hatchets."

What are two reactions the Europeans had toward the Native Americans?

_____

_____

Harcourt Brace School Publishers

Document 2

A Native American described his first sighting of the Europeans with Henry Hudson. It was written down by John Heckewelder in the 1700s as follows:

"[B]ut other runners soon after arriving declare that [Hudson's ship] is positively a house full of human beings, of quite a different color from that of the Indians, and dressed differently from them; that in particular one of them was dressed entirely in red. . . . Many are for running off to the woods, but are pressed by others to stay. . . .

The house . . . at last stops, and a canoe of a smaller size comes on shore with the red man, and some others in it; some stay with his canoe to guard it. The chiefs and wise men, assembled in council, form themselves into a large circle, toward which the man in red clothes approaches with two others. He salutes them with a friendly [face], and they return the salute. . . . They are lost in admiration; the dress, the manners, the whole appearance of the unknown strangers is to them a subject of wonder; but they are particularly struck with him who wore the red coat all glittering with gold lace, which they could in no manner account for."

What are two reactions the Native Americans had toward the Europeans?

_____

_____

Document 3

An excerpt of a letter to the Dutch West India Company from Captain Peter Schaghen.

Yesterday the ship the *Arms of Amsterdam* arrived here [in Europe]. It sailed from New Netherland out of the River Mauritius on the 23rd of September. They report that our people are in good spirit and live in peace. The women also have borne some children there. They have purchased the Island Manhattes from the Indians for the value of 60 guilders. . . . They had all their grain sowed by the middle of May, and reaped by the middle of August. They sent samples of these summer grains: wheat, rye, barley, oats, buckwheat, canary seed, beans and flax. The cargo of the aforesaid ship is:

7246 Beaver skins	178 1/2 Otter skins
675 Otter skins	48 Mink skins
36 Lynx skins	33 Minks
34 Weasel skins	

What does this letter suggest about ways the Europeans and Native Americans

found to get along? _____

_____

PART B: ESSAY RESPONSE

On a separate sheet of paper, write an essay about Native American and European reactions to each other. In your essay, describe how European and Native American views of each other were different and how they were similar. Use the documents and the answers you gave in Part A to help you plan your essay.

In your essay, remember to:

- Identify how Europeans felt and acted toward Native Americans
- Identify how Native Americans felt and acted toward Europeans
- Explain ways in which the two groups cooperated

Harcourt Brace School Publishers

The English Take New York

In March 1664 the king of England, Charles II, gave his brother James, Duke of York a huge amount of land in North America. This land included New England and the Dutch colony of New Netherland. King Charles II ignored the Dutch claim to the land.

James was not only Duke of York but also Lord High Admiral of England. At his order four warships commanded by Colonel Richard Nicolls (NIH•kuhlz) sailed to North America to claim the duke's new colony. The plan was to take over New Amsterdam. On August 26 ships docked near the town. Colonel Nicolls ordered Dutch governor Peter Stuyvesant to give up the town and its fort. Nicolls warned that if the Dutch did not give in within 48 hours, the English troops would take the town.

The colonists, town leaders, and soldiers of New Amsterdam asked Governor Stuyvesant to give up. New Amsterdam was run-down and had little food. Although he did not want

to, Governor Stuyvesant gave in. Colonel Nicolls's troops landed and claimed the town for James, Duke of York and the English. On September 8 Governor

Peter Stuyvesant

Stuyvesant and the Dutch soldiers sailed away from what was now an English territory.

The English promised not to bother the Dutch settlers or force them to move, so most people stayed. They promised to be loyal to the English. Even so, the colony's people and culture remained more Dutch than English for many years. Some changes came quickly, though. The New Netherland colony was renamed New York after the Duke of York. The town of New Amsterdam became the town of New York.

Review

CHECK UNDERSTANDING

1. How did the Dutch colony of New Netherland become the English colony of New York?
2. Why did the people of New Amsterdam want the governor to give in to the English?

THINK CRITICALLY

3. Why do you think the English let the Dutch settlers stay?

SHOW WHAT YOU KNOW

Write a front-page newspaper article about the English takeover of New Netherland. Be sure to include a headline.

Harcourt Brace School Publishers

Activity

Mapping Colonial New York

DIRECTIONS: Study the map below. Then complete the activities.

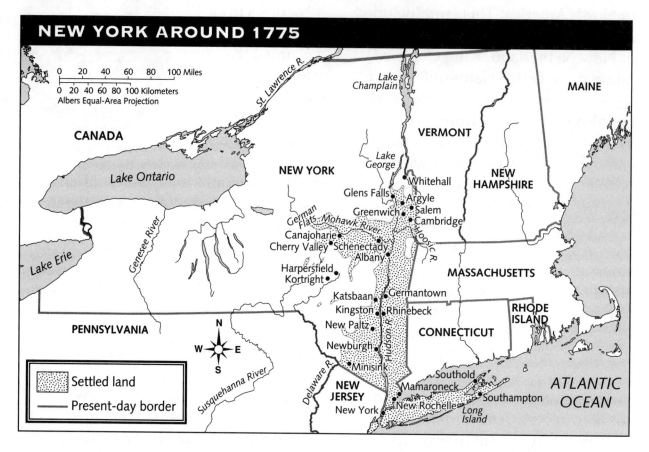

NEW YORK AROUND 1775

1. Put an X at the location of your community. Was the area around your

   community settled by Europeans or unsettled as of 1775? _____

2. Imagine that you are a fur trader traveling by canoe from Schenectady to the town of New York to sell your fur pelts. In a canoe you can travel about 5 miles (8 km) an hour. Trace a water route from Schenectady to New York. Then measure the distance using the map scale.

   About how many miles is your trip? _____

   How long will it take you? _____

3. Imagine you are a merchant traveling by horse from Harpersfield to Albany to sell your goods. A horse can travel 8 miles (13 km) an hour. Trace a land route from Harpersfield to Albany. Then measure the distance using the map scale.

   About how many miles is your trip? _____

   How long will it take you? _____

Harcourt Brace School Publishers

Two Views of Colonial Albany

Two writers visiting Albany in the mid-1700s had different views of the town. The first of the writers to visit was Peter Kalm. He came to Albany in 1749 to study North American plants and animals. Kalm was a Swedish **naturalist**, or a person who studies nature and the environment. Kalm wrote a book about his trip called *Travels in North America*. It is part **travelogue**, or a description of a trip, and part report on North American plants and animals:

"Next to New York Albany is the principal town, or at least the most wealthy, in the province of New York. It is situated on the slope of a hill, close to the western shore of the Hudson River. . . . There are two churches in Albany, one English and the other Dutch. The Dutch church stands a short distance from the river on the east side of the market. It is built of stone and in the middle it has a small steeple with a bell. . . . The English church is situated on the hill at the west end of the market, directly under the fort. It is likewise built of stone but has no steeple. . . .

The houses in this town are very neat, and partly built of stones covered with shingles of white pine. Some are slated with tile from Holland. . . . The front doors are generally in the middle of the houses, and on both sides are porches with seats, on which during fair weather the people spend almost the whole day, especially on those porches which are in the shade. . . . The streets are broad, and some of them paved. In some parts they are lined with trees. The long streets are almost parallel to the river, and the others intersect them at right angles."

Albany, about 1770

(continued)

Harcourt Brace School Publishers

Twenty years later, Richard Smith passed through the town. He too described what he saw. Smith was a lawyer from New Jersey. He traveled to Albany to look at some land he bought in what is today Otsego (aht•SEE•goh) County.

"At Half after 10 o'clock we arrived at Albany. . . . In the afternoon we viewed the Town which contains according to several Gentlemen residing there, about 500 Dwelling Houses besides Stores and Out Houses. The streets are irregular and badly laid out, some paved others not, Two or Three are broad and the rest narrow and not straight. Most of the Buildings are . . . shaped like the old Dutch Houses of New York. . . . There are 4 Houses of Worship for different Denominations and a Public Library which we did not visit. Most of the Houses are built of Brick. . . . The Inhabitants generally speak both Dutch and English . . ."

DIRECTIONS: Complete the chart to compare the two descriptions of Albany.

	Peter Kalm	Richard Smith
Number of Churches		
Building Materials		
Description of Roads		
Other Buildings Mentioned		

Why do you think these writers had such different views of Albany? What may have affected each writer's point of view?

Harcourt Brace School Publishers

Your Community

Early Settlers

DIRECTIONS: Find out about the first European settlement at or near your community. Then use that information to complete the organizer below. In the space on the next page, draw a picture of the oldest building still in use in your community. Write a caption for your picture, telling when the building was built, what it was first used for, and where it is located.

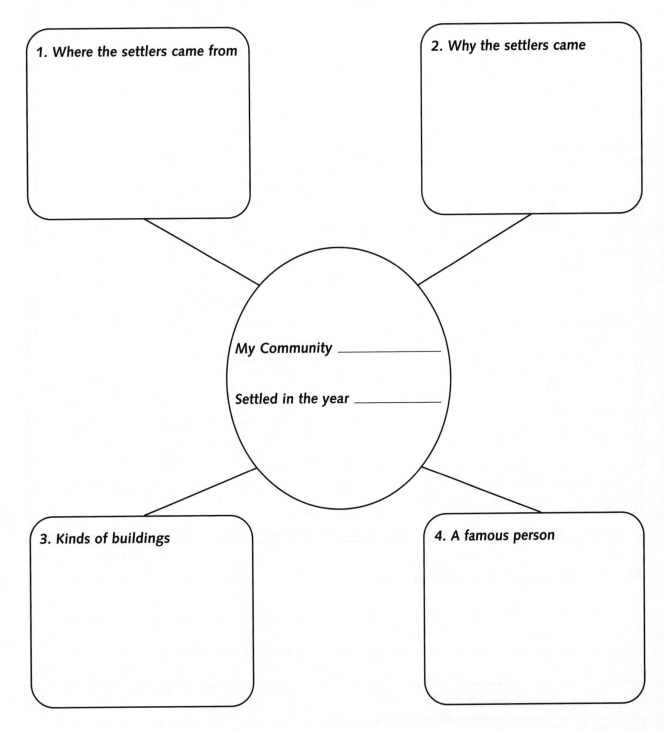

1. Where the settlers came from

2. Why the settlers came

My Community _____

Settled in the year _____

3. Kinds of buildings

4. A famous person

(continued)

Harcourt Brace School Publishers

The oldest building in my community _____

_____

_____

_____

_____

Harcourt Brace School Publishers

Colonial Life in New York

The colony of New York grew slowly at first. In 1664 only about 9,000 people had settled in the colony. About 1,500 people lived in the town of New York. About 300 colonists lived in Albany, the present-day capital of New York State.

The population of colonial New York did not grow quickly for many reasons. The Dutch government had given huge amounts of land to people who then rented small plots to settlers. The new English rulers also tried to do this. However, new settlers did not want to be **tenants**, or renters. Instead, they went to other colonies where they could buy land.

Another reason for New York's small population was war. The French, the British*, and the Native Americans all struggled for control of the central and western parts of the colony. To stay friendly with the Haudenosaunee nations, the British did not allow settlers to move west of what is now the city of Rome, New York. This limited the land available for new settlers to use.

Slowly, the population of New York did grow. By the 1770s the colony had a European population of 175,000. About half its citizens were English and about one-eighth were Dutch. The rest included French, Germans, Scots, Irish, and Swedes. About 20,000 slaves from Africa also lived in the colony.

Colonial New York had a mixed economy. An **economy** is the way

---

*In 1707 England and Scotland signed a treaty called the Act of Union. This agreement united Scotland and England into one country. (Wales had become part of England several hundred years earlier.) Since that time, the nation has been known as Great Britain or Britain. The people of Britain are called the British.

New York Harbor as it looked about 1756

(continued)

Harcourt Brace School Publishers

people use resources to meet their needs. Many New Yorkers farmed for a living. They grew food for themselves. They also sold grain to the other colonies or to Britain. Other New Yorkers worked in the forestry industry. Wooded areas covered much of the colony. The trees in New York's forests were used to make masts for ships, turpentine, and other goods. The trade in these goods helped bring about another New York industry—shipbuilding.

New Yorkers living in cities often became merchants. The excellent harbor of New York City made it a good place for trade. Items such as beeswax, candles, pork, chocolate, and flax for making linen were exported from New York Harbor to Britain, the West Indies, or the other colonies.

If a New Yorker did not work as a farmer, forester, merchant, or sailor, he or she could work at many other jobs. Newspapers were the most popular form of reading material in the colonies. To meet this need, some people became printers. Others made things for everyday use, such as barrels, pottery, saddles, and cloth. Blacksmiths not only made horseshoes but also tools, nails, pots, and pans. Shopkeepers sold food, cloth, candles, tea, coffee, salt, and sugar.

Children in colonial New York usually did not go to school. Only a few rich families could send their children to school. Girls learned how to keep house. Boys worked on the family farm or learned a trade. King's College opened in 1754, but few people were able to go to college. Today King's College is known as Columbia University. It was one of the first and best colleges in the American colonies.

Review

CHECK UNDERSTANDING

1. What two industries were growing in colonial New York?
2. What natural resources did early settlers use most?

THINK CRITICALLY

3. How might having a variety of jobs help a place to grow?

SHOW WHAT YOU KNOW

Choose one of the many colonial New York jobs you learned about in this lesson. Write a paragraph titled "A Day in the Life of a Colonial New Yorker." If you wish, you may use outside resources to find additional information about the job you choose.

Harcourt Brace School Publishers

Activity

Trade in Colonial New York

DIRECTIONS: Study the graphs below. Then answer the questions.

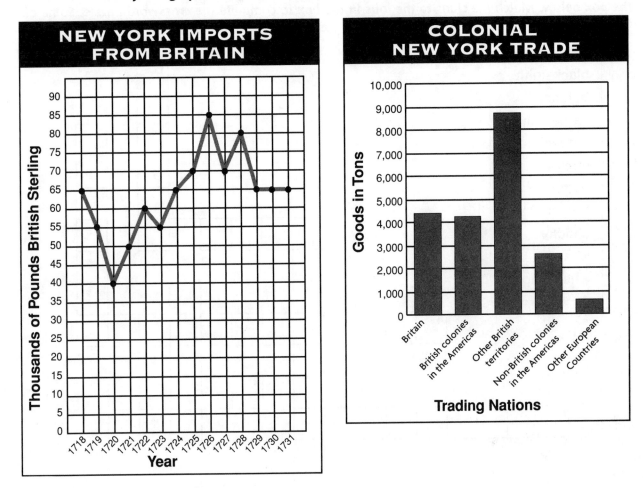

1. In which year did New York import the most goods? _____

2. In which year did New York import the fewest goods? _____

3. What was the value of goods imported for each of the following years?

   1720 _____   1723 _____   1725 _____   1729 _____

4. Which customer traded most with New York? _____

5. About how many tons of goods did Britain trade with New York? _____

6. About how many tons of goods did non-British colonies in the Americas trade

   with New York? _____

Harcourt Brace School Publishers

Activity

Kinds of Work in Colonial New York

DIRECTIONS: *People in colonial New York had many different jobs. Some of these are listed in the box below. Match the clues to the jobs in the box to complete the crossword puzzle. Some of these jobs no longer exist, so you may need to research to solve the clues.*

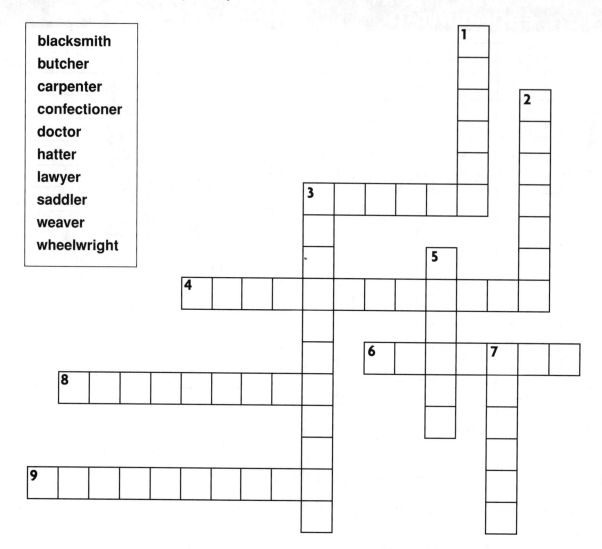

blacksmith
butcher
carpenter
confectioner
doctor
hatter
lawyer
saddler
weaver
wheelwright

ACROSS:

3. a person who makes cloth or baskets
4. a person who makes candy
6. a person who sells meat
8. a person who makes and repairs wooden objects
9. a person who shapes iron with an anvil and hammer

DOWN:

1. a person who represents other people in a court of law
2. a person who makes, sells, and repairs equipment for horses
3. a person who repairs wheels
5. a person who tries to help people who are hurt or sick
7. a person who makes and sells hats

Harcourt Brace School Publishers

Colonial Farm Families

DIRECTIONS: Read the text, and study the picture below. Then choose one food item from the picture, and complete the activities that follow.

Surviving on a farm in colonial New York took much more than clearing the land and planting seeds for grain. Like Native Americans, most farm families lived far from towns or cities. They had to be mostly **self-sufficient**, or able to provide all their needs for themselves. Farm families fished, gathered berries and apples, made jelly, and hunted deer and other animals. If they had a cow, they cared for it, milked it, and made butter and cheese from the milk. Farm families kept food for winter by drying fruits, smoking meats, and making cider.

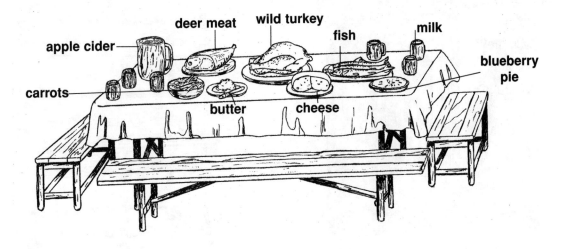

Food Item: _____

1. How did a colonial family get the item you chose? Did they grow it, hunt it, gather it, or make it from cow's milk?

   _____

2. How would your family get the item you chose?

   _____

3. Describe the steps needed to bring food from farm to table today. Be sure to include any pre-cooking, packaging, and a delivery method to bring your food to the store.

   _____

   _____

   _____

   _____

Harcourt Brace School Publishers

Examine Text and Visuals

Made in New York

DIRECTIONS: Read the paragraph, and study the pictures. Then complete the graphic organizer below to compare and contrast the two dressers.

The furniture styles of the Dutch and English settlers of New York were very different but served similar purposes. The Dutch settlers used a **kas,** or cabinet, as a dresser, cabinet, and closet all in one. The kas shown below was made of painted oak and gumwood in about 1720. The English style **highboy,** or tall dresser, was made of gumwood in the late 1600s for a family on Long Island.

Dutch kas, about 1720

English-style highboy, late 1600s

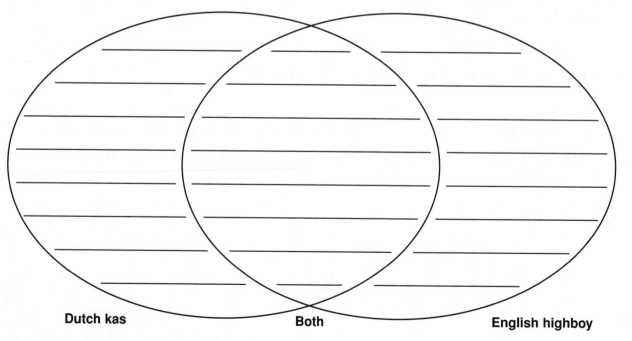

Dutch kas   **Both**   **English highboy**

y

Harcourt Brace School Publishers

Earning a Living

By the late 1700s New York City was a center for businesses of all kinds. Many people earned a living by making and selling products or by providing services. One way a merchant could attract customers was by advertising in colonial newspapers.

DIRECTIONS: Use the library to learn how early settlers in your area supported themselves and their families. Then, on a separate sheet of paper, design an advertisement for a product or service made or provided by early settlers in your community. You may use these advertisements that appeared in colonial newspapers as examples. Note: Printers during this time often used the character ʃ to stand for s.

CHAIR MANUFACTORY

CARRIED ON, By
JAMES CHESTNEY,
No. 72, north end of Market ʃtreet, Albany :
WHERE MAY BE HAD,
COMMON, Windʃor & fancy or Cottage CHAIRS, on the moʃt reaʃonable terms. Alʃo, Chairs made to any pattern, on the ʃhorteʃt notice and on reaʃonable terms.
Old Chairs mended and bottomed. Some Flaggs, Rounds and Slatts for ʃale, ALSO,
Dry Goods & Groceries,
as uʃual—And a freʃh Aʃʃortment of
GARDEN SEEDS,
Wholeʃale and Retail.
☞ As he has ʃuffered much by the late Fire, he hopes that the continuance of the friendʃhip of a generous Public, will in ʃome meaʃure compenʃate for his recent loʃʃes. Thoʃe indebted to him will oblige him much by making immediate payment.
February 19, 1798.   73ᵐ

An advertisement for a chair maker. It tells that Mr. James Chestney will custom-make chairs to any pattern.

SARAH SELLS,
MUFFIN-MAKER, in BROAD-STREET:
TAKES this Method of informing her Friends, and the Publick in general, that ʃhe continues making MUFFINS and CRUMPETS hot twice every Day ; humbly thanks her Friends for their former Favours, and intreats the Continuance of them, which ʃhe will make it her conʃtant Endeavour to deʃerve, and which will be ever gratefully acknowledged.

A baker thanks her customers and asks that they continue to buy her muffins.

Harcourt Brace School Publishers

The Colonial Government of New York

In 1685 New York became a royal colony. As a **royal colony** New York was controlled by the king of England, James II. The king chose a governor to rule the colony with a council of colonists as advisers to him. Still, most New Yorkers had little say in their government.

In January 1683 Governor Thomas Dongan allowed the colonists to elect their own **legislature,** or lawmaking group. This legislature was called the General Assembly. King James II later fired Dongan for giving New York colonists too much power.

The seal used by Royal Governor Thomas Dongan

A short time later, James II decided to unite New York, New Jersey, and New England into one territory. He called it the Dominion of New England and made his friend Edmund Andros governor. Andros had been governor of New York before, and many people did not like him. Now Andros controlled New York again, but this time from Boston, Massachusetts. This upset many New Yorkers. They feared that they would no longer have any voice in decisions.

This fear led to a revolt in 1689. It was named Leisler's Revolt after a rich merchant, Jacob Leisler (LYS•luhr). He and other colonial leaders took charge of the colony. They called for the election of a new General Assembly. Leisler and the assembly ran the colony for almost two years.

During the same year, the people of England removed James II from the throne. The new rulers were Queen Mary and King William. The colonies went back to having separate governors, ending the Dominion of New England. William and Mary sent a new royal governor to New York. Governor Henry Sloughter decided to keep the General Assembly.

Review

CHECK UNDERSTANDING

1. Which colonies were joined to make the Dominion of New England?

2. Who was the leader of the 1689 revolt?

THINK CRITICALLY

3. Why do you think colonial New Yorkers wanted a General Assembly?

SHOW WHAT YOU KNOW

Imagine that you are a colonist living in New York in 1689. Write a letter to a friend telling why you would or would not want New York to be part of the Dominion of New England.

Harcourt Brace School Publishers

The French and Indian War

Between 1689 and 1763 France and Britain battled for land around the world. France claimed a large colony in North America called New France. This land claim included much of what is today Canada and large areas to the south around the Great Lakes and the Ohio and Mississippi River valleys. New France had a small population. Yet its forts and settlements controlled the fur trade with the Native Americans of the area.

Several French forts were located in areas of what is today northern New York State. These included Fort Frederic on Lake Champlain, Fort Niagara (ny•A•gruh) on the Niagara River, and Fort Carillon (KAR•uh•lohn) at Ticonderoga (ty•kon•duh•ROH•guh).

The British also built forts to protect their territory in the New York colony. These forts included Fort Edward on the upper Hudson River, as well as Fort William Henry and Fort George, both on Lake George.

France and Britain were building forts in other areas too. In one such case, the British built a fort in Pennsylvania. As soon as the fort was finished, the French attacked it. The French then built Fort Duquesne (doo•KAYN) on the same spot in 1753. The governor of Virginia sent a young officer named George Washington to force the French to leave.

Powder horn from the French and Indian War showing the names of battles in New York

In April 1754, George Washington and an army of about 150 Virginia soldiers set out for Fort Duquesne. On their way to the fort, Washington and his soldiers met a group of French soldiers. Washington was worried that a larger French army might be nearby. He ordered his soldiers to build a fort quickly. They did so and named it Fort Necessity. In a short time 600 French soldiers arrived and attacked Washington's fort. Although he gave up the fort, Washington earned praise for his bravery.

The defeat of George Washington at Fort Necessity became the first battle in a long war. To the colonists this war was known as the French and Indian War. In Europe it was called the Seven Years' War.

During the earlier conflicts between the French and the British, the Native Americans of the area had remained **neutral**. That is, they did not join either side. In the French and Indian War, the Haudenosaunee nations sided with the British. Some Algonquian nations sided with the French.

(continued)

Harcourt Brace School Publishers

In the first few years of the war, the French won many battles. In 1757 they burned the British fort, William Henry. In July 1758 the British lost one of the worst battles at Ticonderoga. However, a year later Lord Jeffrey Amherst (AM•erst) led the British to victory in several battles in northern New York. The French troops set fire to their own forts as they retreated north.

With all of what is now New York under their control, the British focused on the city of Quebec (kwih•BEK). On September 13, 1759, the British took Quebec from the French.

The Peace of Paris ended the war in 1763. In this treaty, France gave almost all of New France to the British. The British now controlled most of eastern North America.

DIRECTIONS: After reading about the French and Indian War, match the events to the date on which each event occurred. Draw a line from the column labeled Event to the correct date in the second column.

Event		Date
The British capture Quebec.		1753
The treaty known as the Peace of Paris ends the war. France gives almost all of its land in North America to Britain.		1754
The French build Fort Duquesne.		1757
The British lose a major battle at Ticonderoga.		1758
The French destroy Fort William Henry.		1759
The French defeat Washington at Fort Necessity.		1763

Harcourt Brace School Publishers

Learning About Other Colonies

DIRECTIONS: New York was one of 13 British colonies in North America. Choose one of the other 12 colonies to research. Use encyclopedias and other library resources to find the information needed to complete the chart.

The Colony of _____

Date founded	
Name(s) of founders	
Reasons for starting the colony	
Where most of the colony's settlers came from	
When the colony started a legislature or an assembly	
Three other interesting facts about the colony	1. 2. 3.

Harcourt Brace School Publishers

New York Folklore

DIRECTIONS: Read the following stories about New York. Then answer the questions.

Folklore is a collection of stories, songs, and traditions preserved by a group of people over time. Sometimes folktales or songs are called **myths.** Myths tell how something came to be or tell about a clever, brave, or heroic person. Another kind of folklore is called a **legend.** Legends are almost always based on a historical event or person. Unlike history, legends include events that probably did not happen. Following are two examples of New York folklore.

Whisper the Smithtown Bull

More than 300 years ago, some Native Americans offered a challenge to an English settler named Richard Smith who wanted some land. The Native Americans said that Smith could keep whatever land he could circle in a day's time. To make the task more difficult, Smith had to do it riding his bull, Whisper.

Being very clever, Smith waited for the longest day of the year to come. Then, the night before his ride, he trotted an old cow over a 55 mile (88 km) route he had chosen. This was not just any cow—it was Whisper's own mother. Smith thought that Whisper might run faster following his mother's trail.

It worked! By noon Smith and Whisper had traveled so far and so fast that they had time to take a little rest. Smith munched on bread and cheese in a small hollow at the side of the path. Today the road that runs nearby is called Bread and Cheese Hollow Road, in honor of Smith's snack.

Soon, however, Smith and Whisper had to start moving again. It was close, but by the time darkness fell that night, Smith had won his land. He promptly named the area after himself. That is how Smithtown, Long Island, came to be.

Statue of Whisper the Bull

Harcourt Brace School Publishers

(continued)

Captain Billopp and Staten Island

How did Staten Island become part of New York State? When James, Duke of York, gave away the land that became New Jersey, both colonies laid claim to Staten Island.

To solve this sticky problem, James came up with an unusual idea. He said that if a ship could sail around every island of the state's coast in one day, Staten Island would belong to New York. If the ship failed, the island would belong to New Jersey. New Yorkers did not like the idea. It seemed impossible for a ship to make such a journey in a single day.

The people of New York asked Christopher Billopp in his ship the *Bentley* to try to win the island. Captain Billopp had an idea. If he covered the ship's deck with empty barrels, they would catch the wind like extra sails! The *Bentley* would almost fly across the water!

Billopp's plan worked. Not only did he make it around all the islands in one day, he did it with an hour to spare!

The Duke was so amazed by the captain's deed that he rewarded Billopp with a huge estate right on Staten Island. Billopp named his home there the Manor of Bentley, after his ship.

1. List three things in each tale that could be based on historical facts.

_____

_____

_____

2. List three things in each tale that probably did not really happen.

_____

_____

_____

3. Do you think these two stories are myths or legends? Why?

_____

_____

_____

_____

Harcourt Brace School Publishers

The American Revolution

Many American colonists wanted to be free from British rule. They hoped to form their own independent, self-governing nation. The British army met the American army at Lexington, Massachusetts, in April of 1775. There, the first shots of the American Revolution were fired. The fighting continued as both armies moved to the nearby town of Concord. About 60 years later, poet Ralph Waldo Emerson would call the first gunfire at Concord "the shot heard round the world."

New York was the site of several important battles of the revolution. In the first, American soldiers led by Ethan Allen and Benedict Arnold set out to capture Fort Ticonderoga on Lake Champlain from the British. Americans were able to take the fort without much of a fight in May 1775. Up to this point in the war, the American army had a shortage of weapons. Capturing Fort Ticonderoga gave them 78 cannons and thousands of cannonballs.

A year later, in March and April 1776, General George Washington, commander of the American army, thought the British were planning to surround the New England colonies. Washington worried that the British would try to cut New England off from the rest of the colonies. He thought that the British would use New York Harbor as their starting point for an attack. He moved his forces to Long Island to meet the British there.

A soldier in the American army

Washington was right. On July 2, British commander Sir William Howe reached Staten Island. By early August, Howe had gathered about 32,000 soldiers there. By the end of August, his troops had moved to Long Island.

Because General Washington was outnumbered, he and his troops were forced to retreat. The British navy guarded the harbor and rivers. This cut the American army off from the help of the other colonies. In spite of the number of British troops, Washington decided not to give up New York City without a fight.

On August 27 Howe attacked the Americans at Brooklyn Heights, the

(continued)

Harcourt Brace School Publishers

area known today as Prospect Park. It seemed as if the British would capture Washington and his soldiers. However, Howe's troops had not managed to block off the East River. A small group of Massachusetts fishers helped Washington by ferrying his troops across the river from Brooklyn to Manhattan. From there Washington pulled his army back to New Jersey. Howe's troops captured New York City. The city remained under British control for the rest of the war.

The battle for New York weakened the American army. In 1777 the British planned a three-part attack on the Americans. The main part of the British army would push south from Canada through the Hudson River valley. Another group would move east from Oswego through the Mohawk valley. Howe planned to move a third force north on the Hudson River.

The main British army, led by General John Burgoyne (ber•GOYN), easily recaptured Fort Ticonderoga in June. Yet, American attacks slowed his advance southward. British Colonel Barry St. Leger planned to move east from Oswego to meet up with Burgoyne. St. Leger had to retreat after a defeat at Oriskany (awr•IS•kih•nee), near the city of Rome.

Burgoyne did not give up trying to reach Albany. He met the American army in two battles in New York, one at Freedman's Farm on September 19 and the other at Bemis Heights on October 7. The Americans defeated him both times. These victories marked the turning point in the American Revolution.

Burgoyne surrendered at Saratoga on October 13, 1777. His surrender led to the French joining the American cause. With the help of the French people, the American army began winning the war for independence.

Review

CHECK UNDERSTANDING

1. Why did George Washington take his troops to the New York City area in 1776?

2. What were the three parts of the British plan to attack New York in 1777?

THINK CRITICALLY

3. Why might the British have thought that separating the New England colonies from the other colonies would help them win the war?

SHOW WHAT YOU KNOW

On an outline map of New York State, show the three routes the British planned to take to attack New York. Use three different colors to represent the different routes. Be sure to include a map key, telling which route each color represents.

Harcourt Brace School Publishers

Activity

Leaders of the American Revolution

DIRECTIONS: *New York played an important role in the American Revolution. Choose one of the following leaders to research. Fill in the chart below with information you find. Then use that information to design a monument for your leader that focuses on his or her contribution to the American Revolution.*

Ethan Allen	Sybil Ludington	Isaac Sears
Joseph Brant	Richard Montgomery	George Washington
Horatio Gates	Philip Schuyler	Anthony Wayne
Nicholas Herkimer	Margaret Todd Whetten	Jane Cannon Campbell

Name of Leader: _____

	Monument:
Date and place of birth:	
Date and place of death:	
Role in the American Revolution:	

Harcourt Brace School Publishers

Battles of the American Revolution in New York State

DIRECTIONS: Study the map, and answer the questions below.

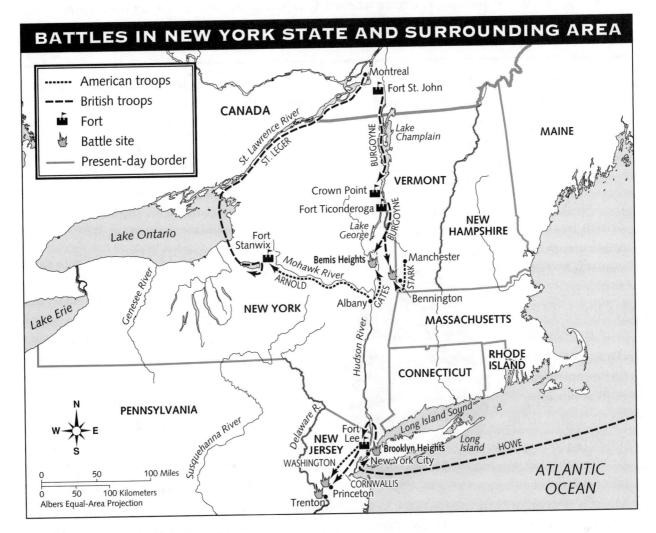

BATTLES IN NEW YORK STATE AND SURROUNDING AREA

1. Where was the battle between Burgoyne and Gates fought?

_____

2. Which river did St. Leger follow to Lake Ontario?

_____

3. At what two places did Washington's and Cornwallis's troops battle?

_____

4. At what fort did St. Leger and Arnold meet?

_____

Harcourt Brace School Publishers

Native Americans and the American Revolution

DIRECTIONS: Read the paragraphs about the role of Native Americans in the American Revolution. Then study each of the quotations. Decide whether the speaker wanted to support the British, support the Americans, or remain neutral. Write British, American, or neutral in the space provided.

When the American Revolution began, the Native Americans of New York tried to remain neutral. However, a Mohawk leader named Joseph Brant convinced many Indian nations to side with the British. Brant had been watching events closely. He saw the British troops force Washington to retreat from New York City. He was sure that the British would defeat the Americans. He wanted to make sure the Native Americans joined the winning side.

Traveling by night Brant made his way past American lines to meet his sister Mary, a powerful clan leader. He and his sister felt that the Americans were taking too much land. They tried to

Mohawk leader Joseph Brant

convince the Haudenosaunee nations to join the British. The Brants told people that they would get to keep their lands. They also told them that they could get back some land they had lost to American colonists.

The Brants convinced the Seneca, Cayuga, and Mohawk nations to fight for the British. The Oneida and Tuscarora nations decided to support the Americans. The Onondaga nation split into three parts. One part supported the British, one part backed the Americans, and one group remained neutral.

When the Indian nations that sided with the British raided villages in New York and Pennsylvania, the Americans responded harshly. They burned Indian crops, orchards, and villages. Some Native Americans fled to Canada, which was still under British control. After the American Revolution ended, many of these people stayed in Canada.

_____ **1.** "We are unwilling to join on either side of such a contest, for we love you both—old England and new."

_____ **2.** "What a wretched situation must you be in when the King attacks all the seaports in America and comes in earnest to sweep off the Americans, if he finds you supporting the Americans."

_____ **3.** "We have now lived in Peace with [the Americans] a long time and we resolve to continue to do so as long as we can."

Harcourt Brace School Publishers

Examine Text and Visuals

West Point Long Ago

DIRECTIONS: Read the paragraph below and study the map. Then answer the questions.

The Hudson River was an important area during the American Revolution. It connected New York to the rest of the colonies. If the British could control the Hudson River, they could easily move troops and weapons from Canada to New York City. For this reason the Americans worked hard to protect the Hudson River. They built up defenses at West Point, a fort near a sharp bend in the river. The fort at West Point was where George Washington established his headquarters in 1789. Today West Point is no longer a fort but a school for men and women who want to be officers in the United States Army.

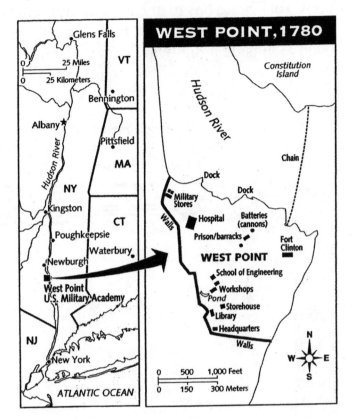

1. What kinds of buildings at West Point were near the Hudson River? Why?

   _____

2. On the map, trace the walls at West Point. Why do you think the walls were placed where they were?

   _____

3. Locate the chain across the Hudson River on the map. Why do you think the Americans put a chain there?

   _____

4. What were two of the buildings at West Point that were not used for a military purpose?

   _____

5. Why might Americans have chosen West Point as a good place for a fort?

   _____

Harcourt Brace School Publishers

Historic Landmarks

Historic monuments and markers remind us of important events and people. New York State has many such monuments and markers. They may be located on the front of a building, in a town square, in local parks or recreational areas, and even alongside a highway. They often include information about the event or person honored, when the event took place, or the contribution of the person and why it was important.

DIRECTIONS: Locate a historical marker in your community. Find or draw a picture of the historical marker, and paste it in the frame below. Then, on a separate sheet of paper, write a paragraph about the marker in your own words.

Harcourt Brace School Publishers

Unit 3 Practice Test

PART I: MULTIPLE-CHOICE

DIRECTIONS: (Questions 1–10) Choose the best answer to each question or incomplete statement. Circle the letter of the answer you choose.

1. In 1664, Colonel Richard Nicolls was sent to North America to

   A take control of New Netherland.

   B become the governor of New England.

   C trade with Native Americans in New York.

   D fight against the Haudenosaunee nations.

2. After Peter Stuyvesant gave up New Amsterdam to the British, the name of the settlement changed to

   A New Jersey.

   B Albany.

   C New York.

   D Rome.

3. How did most people in colonial New York earn a living in the late 1600s?

   A They were trappers.

   B They were printers.

   C They were teachers.

   D They were farmers.

4. In colonial New York, much of the wood taken from the forests was used to

   A make cloth.

   B build ships.

   C make newspapers.

   D weave baskets.

5. Which of the following did New York colonists elect for the first time around 1683?

   A governor of New York

   B members of the General Assembly

   C governor of New England

   D President of the United States

6. Why did Jacob Leisler lead a revolt against the British in 1689?

   A The colonists feared that they had no voice in their government.

   B Leisler did not support the use of slaves.

   C The colonists did not like Governor Donegan.

   D Leisler wanted to take over Haudenosaunee lands.

Harcourt Brace School Publishers

For Questions 7–10, use the time line below.

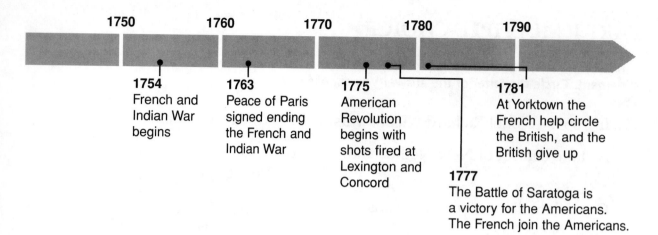

7. How long did the French and Indian War last?

A 10 years   **B** 5 years

C 12 years   **D** 9 years

8. Where did the first battle of the American Revolution take place?

A Lexington and Concord   **B** Yorktown and Williamsburg

C Philadelphia and Pittsburgh   **D** Trenton and Newark

9. What happened soon after the British gave up at Saratoga in 1777?

A The Haudenosaunee nations decided to fight with the Americans.

B General Howe trapped George Washington and his army in New York.

C The French joined the war to help the Americans.

D American soldiers captured Quebec.

10. How long was it from the end of the French and Indian War to the beginning of the American Revolution?

A 10 years   **B** 5 years

C 12 years   **D** 9 years

Harcourt Brace School Publishers

PART II: CONSTRUCTED RESPONSE ITEMS

DIRECTIONS: (Questions 11–20) Write your answer to each question on the lines provided.

For Questions 11–12, use the map below.

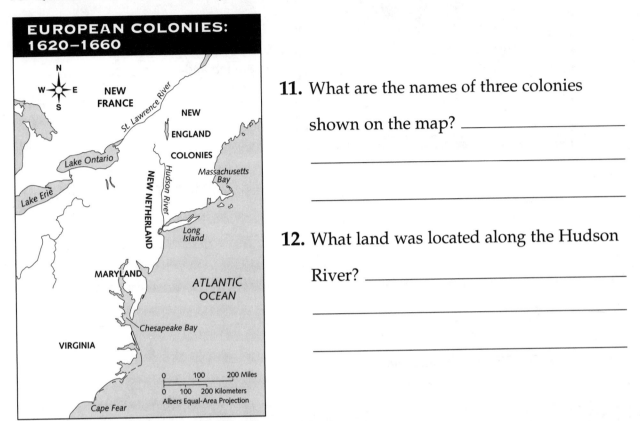

11. What are the names of three colonies shown on the map? _____

_____

_____

12. What land was located along the Hudson River? _____

_____

_____

Read the paragraph below to help answer Questions 13–15.

Before 1664 there were about 9,000 Dutch settlers in the New York colony. There were a number of new English settlers after 1664. Most English colonists chose to buy land rather than rent as tenants. Nearly one-sixth of the population lived in the town of New York. Albany had only about 300 residents. West of Albany, land in the New York colony remained occupied by Haudenosaunee nations. Because the British government wanted to keep good relationships with the Haudenosaunee people, they did not let colonists settle on their lands.

13. Before 1664 most of the European colonists who settled in New York came from which country?

_____

14. Why did English colonists not want to live in New York as tenants?

_____

15. What prevented colonists from settling in western New York?

_____

Harcourt Brace School Publishers

This political cartoon was inspired by Benjamin Franklin during the French and Indian War.

16. What does the cartoon suggest about how the colonists acted during the French and Indian War?

_____

17. What does Franklin's cartoon suggest that he wanted colonists to do?

_____

For Questions 18–20, use the time line below.

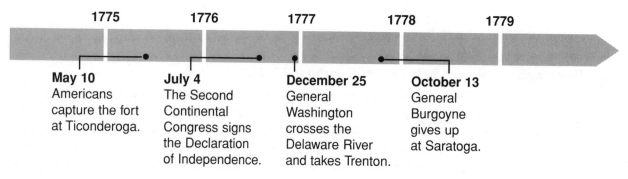

18. In what year did General Burgoyne give up at Saratoga? _____

19. When did George Washington cross the Delaware River? _____

20. Which came first, the signing of the Declaration of Independence or the

capture of the fort at Ticonderoga? _____

Harcourt Brace School Publishers

PART III: DOCUMENT-BASED QUESTIONS

DIRECTIONS: This part of the practice test is designed to find out how well you think and write in social studies.

Historical Background: From 1754 through 1783, France and Britain, along with the American colonists, struggled for control of eastern North America. The Haudenosaunee nations in New York were divided. Some Haudenosaunee nations supported one side or another. Others tried to remain neutral.

Below are some primary sources related to the struggle for control of eastern North America. The first are two maps that show how lands were divided before and after the French and Indian War. The second is a painting of Joseph Brant, along with a paragraph describing his role in the American Revolution. The third is a part of the peace agreement that ended the American Revolution.

Task: Write an essay about the land struggle that took place in North America between 1754 and 1783. In your essay, explain what lands each group lost or gained as a result of these struggles. Use the documents below and the answers you give in Part A to help you write your essay.

PART A: SHORT ANSWER

Look at each document, and answer the questions that follow.

Document 1: Maps of Eastern North America

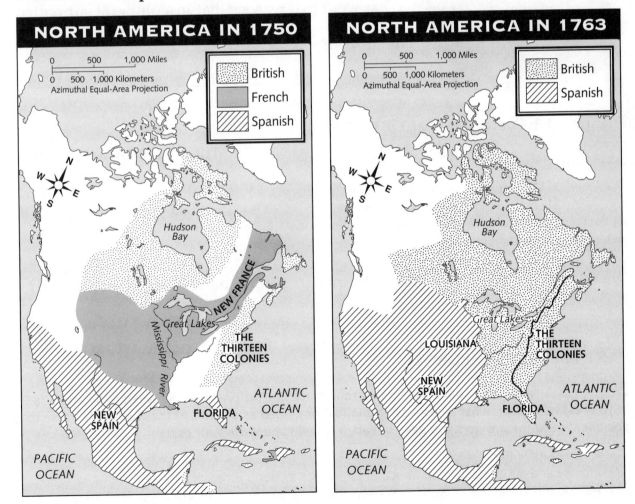

Harcourt Brace School Publishers

What European countries held large amounts of land in North America in 1750?

_____

How did control in North America change in 1763?

_____

_____

Document 2: Portrait of Thayendanegea, a Mohawk, also known as Joseph Brant

At one time, Joseph Brant was an officer in the British army. During the American Revolution, he talked several Haudenosaunee nations into fighting alongside the British. He believed that the British would win the war and the Haudenosaunee nations would be able to keep their lands. Joseph Brant also hoped that the British would return lands that American settlers had taken from the Haudenosaunee people.

What were two reasons that Joseph Brant supported

the British? _____

_____

Document 3: Peace Treaty of 1783

DEFINITIVE TREATY between GREAT BRITAIN and the UNITED STATES of AMERICA, signed at Paris, Sept. 3, 1783.

The American Revolution ended officially with the signing of the Paris Peace Treaty, which included ten articles. Article I stated that Great Britain recognized the United States as an independent nation. Article II set the boundaries of the new nation. The United States took control of all British land south of Canada and east of the Mississippi River.

What lands did the United States of America gain from the Peace Treaty of 1783?

_____

PART B: ESSAY RESPONSE

Write an essay about the land struggle that took place in North America between 1754 and 1783. In your essay, explain what lands each group lost or gained as a result of these struggles. Use the documents and the answers you gave in Part A to help you write your essay.

In your essay, remember to:

- Identify and tell about the two wars that took place in North America between 1754 and 1783
- Identify the European countries, American colonists, and Native American groups that were affected by the struggles
- Discuss the positive results of the land struggles for the United States as a new nation

Harcourt Brace School Publishers

A New Nation

In the mid-1700s King George III and the British Parliament needed money to pay for the French and Indian War. To raise money, Parliament added extra taxes to items that colonists needed such as tea and legal papers. The colonists felt that it was unfair to tax them without a voice in Parliament.

In 1774, leaders in the colonies formed the Continental Congress, a group of representatives from most of the colonies. A **representative** (reh•prih•ZEN•tuh•tiv) is someone chosen by a group of people and given the power to make decisions for them. The Congress met to talk about tax problems. Immediately they voted to stop trade with Britain.

Anger against the British grew. In 1775, Britain and the American colonies began to fight. The American Revolution had begun.

On July 4, 1776, the Continental Congress signed the Declaration of Independence, the document that made the United States a separate nation. It stated the colonists' beliefs in natural **rights**, or freedoms, such as "Life, Liberty, and the pursuit of Happiness."

The Continental Congress began to work on a national government. In 1781 Congress adopted a plan of government called the Articles of Confederation. A **confederation** is a loose alliance based on common interests. Under the articles Congress could ask the states to do certain things, but it could not force them to do anything. This system made the states much stronger than the national government.

The new national government did not work well. Congress could not raise an army or make laws about trade or taxes. New Yorker Alexander Hamilton called for a meeting to talk about the government. In 1787 leaders created a new government under the Constitution of the United States of America.

Sketch of the Great Seal of the United States created in 1789

Review

CHECK UNDERSTANDING

1. What were some of the natural rights stated in the Declaration of Independence?
2. What were some of the problems with the Articles of Confederation?

THINK CRITICALLY

3. Some signers of the Declaration of Independence came from the wealthiest and oldest families in the colonies. Why do you think these men were willing to risk everything to form a new nation?

SHOW WHAT YOU KNOW

Imagine you are living in New York under the Articles of Confederation. Write a letter to the editor of your local newspaper telling why you think a stronger national government is needed.

Harcourt Brace School Publishers

Activity

Patriotic Symbols

There is a long tradition in the United States of using art or cartoons to try to get people to believe in a certain idea or act in a certain way. Sometimes pictures are even better than words for expressing meaning. For example, a school crosswalk sign shows a shaded outline of two children crossing a street between two lines. What is this sign trying to say? If you could not read English, would a sign with words but no picture still manage to deliver the same meaning?

After the American Revolution, political subjects in art were very popular. Americans felt strongly about **patriotism**, or the love of one's country. Ideas that were more difficult to express clearly by writing were often easier using symbols. This painting was made to honor George Washington's leadership and to build trust in the new nation.

DIRECTIONS: Read the paragraphs, and study the picture. Then look at the list of symbols in the box. Write a paragraph on a separate sheet of paper describing how these symbols worked together in the picture to express ideas of good leadership and trust in the government.

A political painting from the 1790s

Eagle with shield, arrows, and olive branch

Star with laurel wreath around the picture

General Washington in his uniform

Scroll showing Independence and July 4, 1776

Marble stand with a message

Banner with a medal

Horns and drums

Flags

Harcourt Brace School Publishers

Community Leaders

DIRECTIONS: *Choose three leaders of your community's government to learn more about.*
Complete the chart with information you find in the library, in the newspaper, or on the Internet.

Name of My Community: _____

Leader 1	Title and Job Description	Leadership Qualities
Leader 2	Title and Job Description	Leadership Qualities
Leader 3	Title and Job Description	Leadership Qualities

Harcourt Brace School Publishers

The Early State of New York

New York State's population and its economy grew rapidly after the American Revolution. These grew mostly because of lands gained after the revolution. Some of the new land came from the property of **Loyalists**, or colonists who supported the British government. Other land came from Native Americans who had moved to **reservations**, or lands set aside by the government.

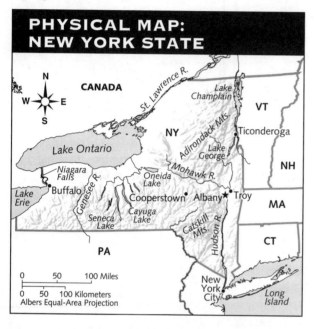

PHYSICAL MAP: NEW YORK STATE

CANADA

St. Lawrence R.

Lake Champlain

VT

NY

Adirondack Mts.

Ticonderoga

Lake George

Lake Ontario

NH

Niagara Falls

Oneida Lake

Mohawk R.

Buffalo

Genesee R.

Cooperstown

Albany

Troy

MA

Lake Erie

Cayuga Lake

Seneca Lake

Catskill Mts.

Hudson R.

CT

PA

New York City

Long Island

0   50   100 Miles
0   50   100 Kilometers
Albers Equal-Area Projection

The state government set aside 1.5 million acres of land for people who had fought in the American Revolution. The land was given out in 600-acre **parcels,** or pieces. Many former soldiers sold their land to people who divided the large parcels and other land into smaller farms. At the same time the state government also sold land at bargain prices.

The large amount of low-cost land attracted many new people to New York State in the early 1800s. **Immigrants**— or people that come to live in a country from their home country—as well as Americans from other states crowded into New York State.

By 1820 New York's population was four times what it was in 1790. New York had more people than any other state in the nation. This quick jump in population helped make the state's economy strong. This, in turn, made New York the nation's leader in manufacturing, banking, and trade by the middle of the 1800s.

Review

CHECK UNDERSTANDING

1. Where did New York State get the land it gained after the American Revolution?
2. Which groups made up the majority of newcomers to New York in the early 1800s?

THINK CRITICALLY

3. Why do you think more people and more land help an economy grow?

SHOW WHAT YOU KNOW

Immigrants have many choices to make about where and how they live. Imagine you are moving to New York in the early 1800s from another state or country. Would you rather live in a city, in a town, or on a farm? What sort of job will you do? Write a paragraph explaining your answer.

Harcourt Brace School Publishers

Activity

Settling Cooperstown

New Yorker William Cooper made a lot of money after the American Revolution. In 1786 Cooper bought 40,000 acres of land. He divided and sold this land to hundreds of settlers. The new landowners clustered around the southern shore of Otsego (ot•SEE•go) Lake. The settlement of Cooperstown was named for William Cooper. He bragged that Cooperstown was the first frontier town of the new nation. The map shows the plan of Cooperstown in 1804. The house in the center of town is Otsego Hall, the home that Cooper built between 1796 and 1799.

DIRECTIONS: Study the map. Then, on a separate sheet of paper, answer the following questions.

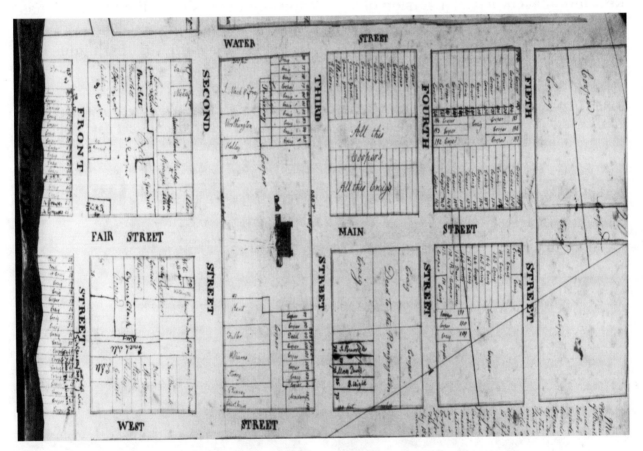

Cooperstown, 1804

1. What were the names of four of the streets in Cooperstown?

2. Why do you think the planner of Cooperstown chose the street names he did?

3. Find Otsego Hall. How would you describe its location?

4. The map shows that most of the lots in Cooperstown were long and narrow. Because of this, the owners could not raise crops. Cooper claimed that people who lived in Cooperstown could not be "half tradesmen and half farmer." Why might Cooper have felt this way?

Harcourt Brace School Publishers

Baseball: An American Pastime

Cooperstown, New York, is the home of the National Baseball Hall of Fame and Museum. The museum opened in 1939, but Americans were playing baseball long before that. New Yorkers read about baseball as early as 1762 in a popular book titled *A Little Pretty Pocket-Book.* Soldiers of the American Revolution even played a version of the game at Valley Forge in 1778.

Baseball has seen many changes over the years. When Brooklyn poet Walt Whitman played the game in the 1820s, players threw the ball at runners and had to hit them to make an out. In 1845 New Yorker Alexander Cartwright rewrote the rules of the game so that the runner would have to be tagged instead of hit by a flying ball.

The Baseball Hall of Fame has a museum that shows how baseball has changed over the years. The museum also has an exhibit that highlights the game's greatest players.

DIRECTIONS: Study the New York Yankee baseball uniforms. On a separate sheet of paper, make a list of ways in which the Yankee uniform has changed from 1912 to the present day. With these changes in mind, design a uniform for the year 2100.

Babe Ruth

David Justice

Harcourt Brace School Publishers

Your Community

Map Your Community

DIRECTIONS: Draw a map of the center of your community similar to the one shown below. Label the important buildings, such as schools, the town or city hall, the police and fire stations, the library, and any parks. Also label main streets and any other places you think are important to your community.

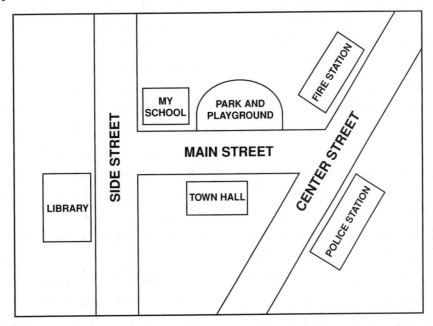

Name of My Community: _____

Harcourt Brace School Publishers

Leaders of the New Nation

In 1787, fifty-five state leaders met in Philadelphia, Pennsylvania, to talk about problems with the national government. These state leaders were **delegates**, or representatives, for citizens of their state. New York sent Alexander Hamilton, John Lansing Jr., and Robert Yates. At this meeting, called the Constitutional Convention, delegates formed a new national government. They did this by writing the Constitution of the United States of America.

The delegates were some of the smartest, best-educated, and most successful people of their time. Some were politicians. Others were lawyers, church leaders, merchants, or gentleman farmers. A few, like the famous Virginian George Washington, had fought in the American Revolution. The delegates decided that Washington should be the convention's president.

Another Virginian, James Madison, played an important role in the creation of the new government. He had many good ideas and kept careful notes of all that happened at the convention. His notes give a record of events that led to the writing of the Constitution.

Madison thought that the government up to this point had failed. Each state had been working only for its own good. Madison believed that a strong central government was necessary to meet the needs of all the states and help them work together.

Other delegates also had new ideas. Alexander Hamilton called for the establishment of a national court. He also suggested that senators should serve for life. Many delegates disliked Hamilton's ideas. Yet Hamilton impressed Madison. Some of his ideas found a place in the Constitution.

Hamilton was the only New Yorker to sign the Constitution. The other New York delegates, Lansing and Yates, left the convention early. They thought that the Constitution gave the national government too much power. They hoped that leaving would make other delegates see their point of view. Instead, delegates who wanted a strong central government won.

Review

CHECK UNDERSTANDING

1. What did James Madison think was wrong with the government?
2. What were some of Alexander Hamilton's ideas for the new government?

THINK CRITICALLY

3. What do you think are three qualities of a good leader?

SHOW WHAT YOU KNOW

Think about the qualities that you listed in Question 3. Then write a short speech called "What Makes a Good Leader?" Present your speech to your classmates.

Harcourt Brace School Publishers

George Washington Arrives in New York City

DIRECTIONS: Read the following paragraphs, and study the picture. Then write the underlined words on a separate sheet of paper. Use clues from the surrounding words and sentences to help define the underlined words. Next, write your own definitions for each word. You may wish to use a dictionary to check your answers.

On April 30, 1789, George Washington stood on the balcony of Federal Hall in New York City. There, he made a short speech called the Presidential oath of office. Washington promised to protect the country's new Constitution. When he had made that promise, George Washington was **inaugurated,** or sworn in, as the first President of the United States of America. Washington arrived in New York by boat a few days earlier, with New Jersey leader Elias Boudinot (ee•LY•uhs BOO•duh•noh). The paragraphs below are from a letter in which Boudinot describes the welcome New Yorkers gave Washington.

"It was with difficulty a passage could be made by the troops through the <u>pressing</u> crowds, who seemed to be <u>incapable</u> of being <u>satisfied</u> by gazing at this man of the people [Washington]. . . .

The streets were lined with the <u>inhabitants</u> as thick as the people could stand. . . . The houses were filled with gentlemen and ladies, the whole distance being half a mile, and the windows to the highest stories were <u>illuminated</u> by the sparkling eyes of <u>innumerable</u> companies of ladies, who seemed to <u>vie</u> with each other to show their joy on this great occasion."

Washington's inauguration at Federal Hall in New York City, 1789

Harcourt Brace School Publishers

John Jay, New York Leader

DIRECTIONS: Read the biography. Then copy the time line below onto a separate sheet of paper. Fill in the blanks with information about John Jay's life and career.

BIOGRAPHY *John Jay, 1745–1829*

Born in New York City on December 12, 1745, John Jay grew up in Rye, New York, and attended King's College. After college, he began a successful law career and married Sarah Van Brugh Livingston. At first, Jay was a Loyalist, but British actions against the colonists upset him. Soon he began to support the American colonists.

John Jay

Jay was a gifted speaker, so New Yorkers chose him to represent them at the Continental Congress in 1774. In 1776 Jay worked hard to get New York State to approve the Declaration of Independence. He also helped write the first New York State Constitution in 1777. In that same year, Jay became the state's first chief justice. A **chief justice** is the head judge in a court that has more than one judge.

In 1782 Jay helped create the Treaty of Paris that ended the American Revolution the next year. Because of his work on this treaty, Jay became the United States Secretary of Foreign Affairs in 1784. In this role he kept good relationships between the United States and other countries.

Jay believed in the ideas stated in the Declaration of Independence. He spoke out against slavery because he felt that liberty should be for everyone. Many New Yorkers agreed with him. In 1785 Jay, Alexander Hamilton, and others formed a group to work towards freeing the slaves. It was so important to Jay that he became the first president of the new anti-slavery group.

Jay did not go to the Constitutional Convention. Yet Jay supported the new Constitution. In 1787 Jay, Hamilton, and James Madison wrote a collection of essays called *The Federalist* papers. These essays helped convince Americans that the new Constitution was needed.

President George Washington made Jay the nation's first chief justice in 1789. Jay was now the leader of the United States Supreme Court but soon left to become a senator from New York.

Washington called upon Jay once again to meet with the British to help prevent another war. Jay did his duty by creating a trade agreement known as Jay's Treaty in 1794. Sadly, many Americans disliked the treaty. Some people even called Jay a traitor. A **traitor** is someone who works against his or her own country.

New Yorkers believed in Jay. In 1795 he was elected governor of New York. He retired from that office in 1801. Jay quietly lived the rest of his life on his farm in Bedford, New York, where he died on May 17, 1829.

Harcourt Brace School Publishers

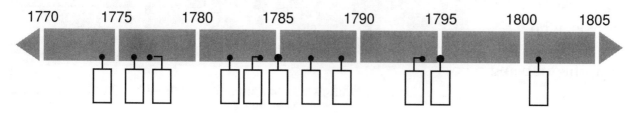

New York Debates the Constitution

For months the people of New York argued over whether to pass the United States Constitution. Many New Yorkers wrote essays either for or against **ratifying,** or accepting, it. Finally, the state approved it in 1788. Below are excerpts, or parts, from two of the many essays and letters written during this time.

New York Governor George Clinton wrote this newspaper article against the Constitution:

"Whoever seriously considers the immense extent of territory comprehended within the limits of the United States . . . will receive it as . . . truth, that a consolidated republican form of government therein, can never form a perfect union. . . . Political liberty is best obtained in moderate governments."

immense: very large
comprehended: included
consolidated: united
republican: representative
moderate: small

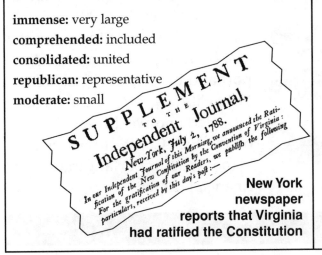

SUPPLEMENT TO THE Independent Journal, New-York, July 2, 1788.
In our Independent Journal of this Morning, we announced the Ratification of the New Constitution by the Convention of Virginia: For the gratification of our Readers, we publish the following particulars, received by this day's post :—

New York newspaper reports that Virginia had ratified the Constitution

New York leader John Jay wrote this essay in favor of the Constitution:

"It has often given me pleasure to observe, that independent America was not composed of detached and distant territories, but [is] one connected, fertile, wide-spreading country.

This country and its people seem to have been made for each other an inheritance so proper and convenient [that it] should never be split into a number of unsocial, jealous, and alien sovereignties.

To all general purposes we have uniformly been one people; each individual citizen everywhere enjoying the same national rights, privileges, and protection. . . ."

inheritance: something passed down over time
convenient: easy
alien: unfamiliar to each other
sovereignties: independent countries

DIRECTIONS: *Copy the following chart onto a separate sheet of paper. In the first column, write the main idea of Clinton's essay. In the second column, write the main idea of Jay's essay. In the bottom box, write a short opinion stating which person you agree with and why.*

Clinton's Main Idea	Jay's Main Idea
My Opinion and Why:	

Harcourt Brace School Publishers

The American Identity

In spite of efforts to maintain peaceful relations with Britain, the United States went to war again. The War of 1812 was caused by trade disagreements between the United States and Britain. When the war ended in victory for the United States, Americans felt proud. The period was known as the Era of Good Feelings. The United States began to develop its own identity.

American literature took on its own style of writing. Two writers of the new literature were New Yorkers. Washington Irving was born in New York City and James Fenimore Cooper grew up in Cooperstown.

Irving wrote stories that were often funny and sometimes scary. In "The Legend of Sleepy Hollow," a school teacher named Ichabod Crane is haunted by a Headless Horseman. "Rip Van Winkle" is about a farmer in the Catskill mountains who fell asleep for 20 years.

Cooper wrote about life on the American frontier. His stories told of Native Americans and life in the wilderness, mostly along the Hudson River. The *Leatherstocking Tales* are a collection of five novels following the life of the original American frontier hero.

By 1815 the frontier had shifted westward to the Mississippi and Ohio river valleys. Six new western states joined the United States in the early 1800s. Still, many people chose to stay in the east building America's great port and industrial cities. New York City was one of the most crowded and wealthiest cities on the East Coast. It was, as it is today, an important trade and financial center.

A busy New York City street in the 1830s

Review

CHECK UNDERSTANDING

1. Why was this period called the Era of Good Feelings?

2. Which American author wrote about life in the New York wilderness?

THINK CRITICALLY

3. Why do you think a period of peace helped the United States to develop its own identity?

SHOW WHAT YOU KNOW

Using pictures and words, create a collage showing the American identity today.

Harcourt Brace School Publishers

New Yorkers Who Made a Difference

DIRECTIONS: *Many New Yorkers contributed to the state and national identity in important ways. Below is a list of some outstanding New Yorkers. Choose a person from the list to learn more about. Use library or internet sources to complete the activities about the person you selected. Then make a poster telling why that person made a difference.*

Edith Wharton	Walt Whitman	John Peter Zenger
Grover Cleveland	Robert R. Livingston	Dewitt Clinton
Frederick Douglass	Aaron Copland	George Clinton
Arthur Tappan	Henry Highland Garnet	Charles Evans Hughes
Gertrude Whitney	Hillary Rodham Clinton	Franklin D. Roosevelt
Susan B. Anthony	Julia Ward Howe	Belva Lockwood
James Baldwin	Theodore Roosevelt	Ely Samuel Parker
Elizabeth Cady Stanton	Gertrude Ederle	George Gershwin
William H. Seward	Lena Horne	Agnes de Mille
Sojourner Truth	John Davison Rockefeller	Herman Melville
Emma Hart Willard	Grandma Moses	William Schuman
Millard Fillmore	Cornelius Vanderbilt	Martin Van Buren
Ira Aldridge	Jonas E. Salk	John Jacob Astor

Name of famous New Yorker:

_____

When did he or she live?

_____

What is this person famous for?

_____

Why is what this person did important?

_____

_____

How has this person affected others?

_____

_____

Harcourt Brace School Publishers

Activity

Population Growth in Early New York

Directions: Use the information in the table to complete the bar graph showing the population of New York State between 1790 and 1850. Then answer the questions below.

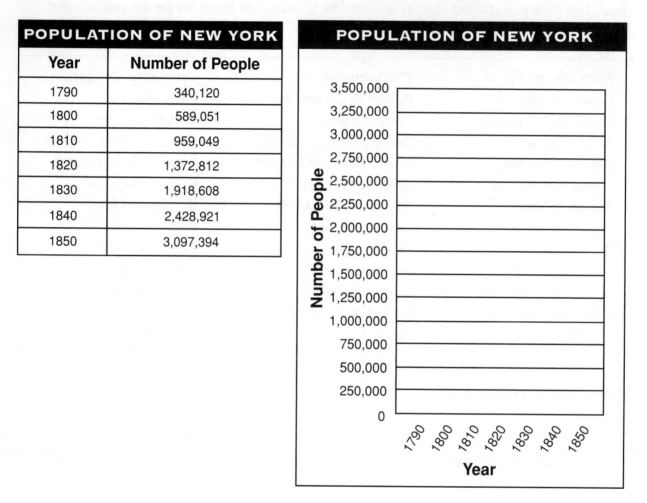

POPULATION OF NEW YORK	
Year	**Number of People**
1790	340,120
1800	589,051
1810	959,049
1820	1,372,812
1830	1,918,608
1840	2,428,921
1850	3,097,394

1. In which ten-year period did population grow the most? _____

2. In which ten-year period did population grow the least? _____

3. What does the bar graph show about the population of New York in the first half of the 1800s?

_____

_____

Harcourt Brace School Publishers

Unit 4 Practice Test

PART I: MULTIPLE-CHOICE

DIRECTIONS: (Questions 1–10) Choose the best answer to each question or incomplete statement. Circle the letter of the answer you choose.

1. Which document established the first national government of the United States?

   A Mayflower Compact

   B the Magna Carta

   C Treaty of Paris

   D Articles of Confederation

2. Which of the following was a problem with the United States's first form of government?

   A Congress could not raise an army or make laws about taxes.

   B The country could not form new states.

   C The central government was too powerful.

   D The British could take control of the colonies.

3. What happened to New York's population after the American Revolution?

   A It decreased because many people died in the war.

   B It stayed the same.

   C It grew rapidly because many new people moved in.

   D It decreased a little because people moved away.

4. New lands available in New York State after the American Revolution mainly came from

   A parts of Canada.

   B Native Americans and Loyalists.

   C parts of Massachusetts.

   D French territories.

5. Where was George Washington sworn in as president in 1789?

   A Washington, D.C.

   B Philadelphia

   C New York City

   D Boston

6. Which of the following delegates at the Constitutional Convention was from New York?

   A George Washington

   B Alexander Hamilton

   C James Madison

   D Benjamin Franklin

Harcourt Brace School Publishers

7. *The Federalist* papers were written to

A convince Americans to ratify the Constitution.

B establish a national court.

C guarantee certain rights for all Americans.

D protect Americans from high taxes.

8. John Jay helped write two treaties that established peace with

A France.

B Native Americans.

C Britain.

D the people of Canada.

Use the table below to answer Questions 9–10.

FAMOUS NEW YORKERS		
Person	**Dates**	**Accomplishments**
James Fenimore Cooper	1789–1851	Author of the *Leatherstocking Tales*
William Cooper	1754–1809	Founder of the first frontier town, Cooperstown
Washington Irving	1783–1859	Author of *The Legend of Sleepy Hollow*
Herman Melville	1819–1891	Author of *Moby Dick*
Elizabeth Cady Stanton	1815–1902	Women's rights activist
Walt Whitman	1819–1892	Poet and author

9. Which person wrote *The Legend of Sleepy Hollow*?

A James Fenimore Cooper

B Walt Whitman

C Elizabeth Cady Stanton

D Washington Irving

10. How did William Cooper contribute to the development of New York State?

A He drew the plans for New York City.

B He fought for women's rights to vote and to own property.

C He wrote a new set of rules for baseball.

D He built the "first frontier town."

Harcourt Brace School Publishers

PART II: CONSTRUCTED RESPONSE ITEMS

DIRECTIONS: (Questions 11–20) *Write your answer to each question on the lines provided.*

Read the following excerpts. Then answer Questions 11–13

Excerpts from The Articles of Confederation, written by the Continental Congress in 1777.

Article I. The [name] of this Confederacy shall be "The United States of America."

Article II. Each state [keeps] its sovereignty, freedom, and independence, and every power, jurisdiction, and right, which is not by this Confederation expressly [given] to the United States, in Congress assembled.

Article V. For the . . . management of the [common] interests of the United States, delegates shall be annually appointed in such a manner as the legislatures of each State shall direct, to meet in Congress on the first Monday in November, in every year . . .

No State shall be represented in Congress by less than two, nor more than seven members; and no person shall be capable of being a delegate for more than three years in any term of six years. . . . In [deciding] questions in the United States in Congress assembled, each State shall have one vote.

11. Under the Articles of Confederation, how were representatives chosen?

_____

12. When were the representatives to meet? _____

13. How many representatives was each state allowed? _____

For Questions 14–15, use the table below.

U.S. POPULATION: 1770–1800				
Colony/State	**1770**	**1780**	**1790**	**1800**
Massachusetts	235,300	268,600	379,000	423,000
New York	162,900	210,500	340,120	589,051
North Carolina	197,200	270,100	394,000	478,000
Pennsylvania	240,100	327,300	434,000	602,000
Virginia	447,000	538,000	692,000	808,000

14. In 1770, what was New York's rank in population compared to the

populations of other colonies shown on the table? _____

15. New York had the third-largest population in 1800. Which two places had

larger populations? _____

Harcourt Brace School Publishers

For Questions 16–18, read the paragraph below. Then fill in the chart by describing how each person helped to form and support a new government.

In 1787, James Madison, Alexander Hamilton, and John Jay all worked to help create and support the new national government. All three wrote a collection of essays called *The Federalist* papers. These essays helped convince Americans that the new Constitution was needed. President George Washington made Jay the nation's first chief justice of the Supreme Court. Alexander Hamilton was chosen as secretary of the treasury. James Madison was responsible for many of the compromises that made up the Constitution and kept the only complete records of the Convention. He is often called the "Father of the Constitution".

	Leader	Contribution
16.	James Madison	
17.	Alexander Hamilton	
18.	John Jay	

For Questions 19–20, read the timeline below.

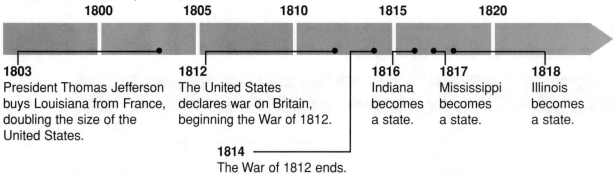

1800 1805 1810 1815 1820

1803
President Thomas Jefferson buys Louisiana from France, doubling the size of the United States.

1812
The United States declares war on Britain, beginning the War of 1812.

1816
Indiana becomes a state.

1817
Mississippi becomes a state.

1818
Illinois becomes a state.

1814
The War of 1812 ends.

19. What two major events happened between 1803 and 1815?

_____

_____

20. What new states were added between 1800 and 1820?

_____

_____

Harcourt Brace School Publishers

PART III: DOCUMENT BASED QUESTIONS

DIRECTIONS: This part of the practice test is designed to find out how well you think and write in social studies.

Historical Background: In 1777 members of the Continental Congress wrote a plan of government called the Articles of Confederation. This new government took effect in 1781 but did not last long. In 1787 representatives from all 13 states met in Philadelphia and wrote a new plan called the Constitution of the United States.

Below are two tables related to the forming of a central government in the United States. The first describes how powers were divided between Congress and the states under the Articles of Confederation. The second table tells how the powers of the central government are separated under the Constitution of the United States.

Task: Write an essay in which you compare and contrast the central government of the United States under the Articles of Confederation and under the United States Constitution. Describe how the two governments are alike and how they are different. Use the tables below and the answers you give in Part A to help you write your essay.

PART A: SHORT ANSWER

Look at each table and answer the questions that follow.

Table 1: The Articles of Confederation

Under the Articles of Confederation, the new government was led by Congress, but the states held most of the power. A president was chosen by a committee to manage the government when Congress was not in session. The table below shows the powers of Congress and the states.

Congress	States
Write laws	Enforce laws
Determine the costs of government	Collect taxes
Declare war	Raise an army and navy
Make treaties with other nations	Control trade between states

Under the Articles of Confederation, what powers did Congress have?

_____

_____

What problem might have occurred if Congress wanted to declare war but the states did not support it?

_____

_____

Harcourt Brace School Publishers

Table 2: The United States Constitution

The Constitution established a new government with three branches. This table describes the powers held by each branch.

Legislative Congress: Senate and House of Representatives	Executive President	Judicial Supreme Court
Makes laws	Manages the government	Interprets the meaning of the laws and treaties
Sets taxes	Enforces laws	
Approves treaties	Makes treaties	
Declares war	Commands armed forces	

How is the President's job under the Constitution different from the President's job under the Articles of Confederation?

_____

_____

PART B: ESSAY RESPONSE

On a separate sheet of paper, write an essay in which you compare and contrast the central government of the United States under the Articles of Confederation and under the United States Constitution. Use the tables and the answers you gave in Part A to help you plan your essay.

In your essay, remember to:
- Identify some of the powers of Congress under the Articles of Confederation
- Identify some of the powers of Congress under the United States Constitution
- Describe some of the powers of the individual states under the Articles of Confederation
- Explain ways in which the states were less powerful under the Constitution
- Describe the three branches of government under the Constitution and tell what powers each branch has.

Harcourt Brace School Publishers

Unit 4

New Ways to Travel

In August 1807 Robert Fulton first introduced a boat powered by a steam-run engine. Fulton's new steamboat the *Clermont* traveled on the Hudson River from New York City to Albany and back again. For the first time a boat moved almost as fast going against a river's current as it had going with the current. Fulton's invention made travel on waterways the fastest way to get from place to place.

Still, rivers did not always run where Americans or their products needed to go. To solve this problem, engineers began to plan and build canals. **Canals** are shallow human-made waterways that connect bodies of water to one another.

One of the most famous canals in the world is the Erie Canal. New Yorkers built it to connect the city of Buffalo on Lake Erie with the city of Albany on the Hudson River. With the canal people and products traveled from midwestern states to the port of New York City much faster and for less money than ever before.

Soon steam-run trains traveling on railways appeared. Trains were much faster than horses. It was not long before railroads became the number-one way to travel and ship goods. Steam-run trains traveled 20 miles an hour (32 kph)—twice the speed of any other kind of transportation.

Inventions such as the steamboat and railroad were part of a larger change in society. During the late 1700s and early 1800s, many new inventions changed the way people lived, worked, and traveled. This period of time has become known as the **Industrial Revolution.**

A train nicknamed the *Iron Horse* defeats a horse-drawn cart in 1830.

Review

CHECK UNDERSTANDING

1. Why was the invention of the steamboat important?
2. How did canals affect early transportation of goods and people?

THINK CRITICALLY

3. Why do you think the Erie Canal helped New York City to grow?

SHOW WHAT YOU KNOW

Imagine that you are a passenger traveling for the first time on a new railroad. Write a letter to a friend telling about your journey. Explain why you chose to take the train instead of a steamboat or horse-drawn coach.

Harcourt Brace School Publishers

The Erie Canal

DIRECTIONS: Read the following paragraphs and song lyrics about the Erie Canal. Then write your own verse for the song.

In 1817 New York Governor DeWitt Clinton suggested building the Erie Canal. When it was done, the canal stretched 363 miles (584 km). It was 40 feet (12.2 m) wide and 4 feet (1.2 m) deep. The canal's shallowness suited the flat-bottomed boats called barges that were pulled by mules walking alongside the canal.

The opening of the Erie Canal on October 25, 1825, meant that people and products could now travel more easily. The canal brought about economic growth in New York State. As time passed, the Erie Canal was widened to 70 feet (21.3 m) and deepened to 7 feet (2.1 m) so that steam-run boats and large barges could use it.

The Erie Canal has remained one of the main transportation routes for products across the state despite the growth of railroads. Today the Erie Canal can support barges carrying up to 2,000 tons.

Low Bridge, Everybody Down

Verse:
I've got a mule, her name is Sal,
Fifteen miles on the Erie Canal.
She's a good ol' worker and a good ol' pal,
Fifteen years on the Erie Canal.
We've hauled some barges in our day,
Filled with lumber, coal, and hay,
And now we know ev'ry inch of the way
From Albany to Buffalo.

Chorus:
Low bridge, ev'rybody down!
Low bridge, for we're comin' to a town!
And you'll always know your neighbor,
You'll always know your pal,
If you've ever navigated on the Erie Canal.

The *Seneca Chief* was the first boat to travel on the Erie Canal.

My verse:

_____ _____

_____ _____

_____ _____

_____ _____

_____ _____

Harcourt Brace School Publishers

Examine Text and Visuals

The Cookstove

Many inventions in the early 1800s made family life easier. One of these was the cookstove. Before 1820 most Americans cooked in fireplaces that needed armloads of wood. Large pots and kettles sat on the **hearth**—the floor of the fireplace—or hung from a swinging rack. Lifting these heavy pots was hard work for the person doing the cooking. Controlling the heat of the fire was also difficult.

In 1820 new ways to manufacture iron helped make safe cookstoves possible. Because of controlled heat and a flat cooking surface on top, people could use pots and pans that did not weigh as much. The stoves also used less wood than fireplaces. New cookstoves first appeared in the homes of the wealthy. By 1850 almost all New Yorkers had a cookstove in their home.

DIRECTIONS: *Imagine that you are a salesperson trying to sell a new cookstove to someone who has never used one. Use facts from the text and the picture above to complete the list of selling points below.*

1. Cookstoves are cleaner than fireplaces because

_____

2. Cookstoves are safer than fireplaces because

_____

3. Cookstoves are easier to use than fireplaces because

_____

4. Cookstoves are cheaper to use than fireplaces because

_____

5. Cookstoves are more modern than fireplaces because

_____

Harcourt Brace School Publishers

Activity

Samuel Morse and the Telegraph

DIRECTIONS: Read the paragraphs, and study the key for Morse code. Use the key to complete the activities below.

Advances were made not just in transportation but also in communication. Samuel Morse, a teacher at the University of the City of New York, began work on an electric telegraph in 1835. A **telegraph** is a machine that sends a series of coded signals from one place to another through wires. Morse believed that this machine would improve

Morse's telegraph

communication by allowing messages to travel as fast as electric current.

In 1838 Morse created a system of dots and dashes to stand for each letter of the alphabet, numbers, and some punctuation marks. His system became known as **Morse code**. It was a huge success. People began to use Morse's machines to send messages all over the world.

Morse Alphabet

A	B	C	D	E	F	G	H	I	J	K	L	M
.-	-...	-.-.	-..	.	..-.	--.	....	..	.---	-.-	.-..	--

N	O	P	Q	R	S	T	U	V	W	X	Y	Z
-.	---	.--.	--.-	.-.	...	-	..-	...-	.--	-..-	-.--	--..

Morse Numbers

0	1	2	3	4
-----	.----	..---	...--	....-

5	6	7	8	9
.....	-....	--...	---..	----.

Morse Punctuation

period	.-.-.-
question mark	..--..
comma	--..--
apostrophe	.----.
quotation mark	.-..-.

1. Decode the message. (Hint: It is the New York State motto.)

.   -.-.   -..   .   ..-.   ..   ..   ---   -..

___ ___ ___ ___ ___ ___ ___ ___ ___

2. Write your name in Morse code.

Harcourt Brace School Publishers

Activity

Changes in New York Roads

DIRECTIONS: Read the following paragraphs, and study the maps showing highways, or major roads, of New York State in 1840 and today. Then complete the activities.

In the early 1800s the United States government began to provide money for a National Road. Over the next 50 years, this road expanded until it stretched from Cumberland, Maryland to Vandalia, Illinois.

During this same time, state governments began to help pay for new state roads. They gave private companies money to build main roads in their own states. New York's state government built three main roads for the state of New York in the 1800s.

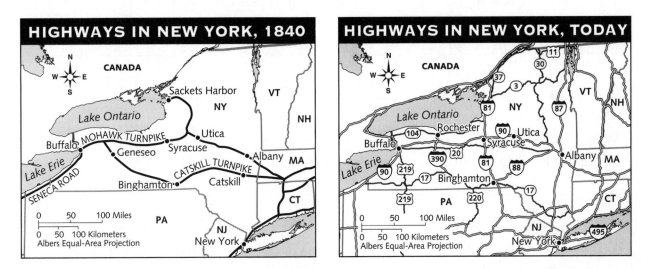

1. Write the numbers of the two present-day highways that follow nearly the same route as the Albany to Sackets Harbor highway did in 1840.

   _____

2. On the map of today, trace the route of the Catskill Turnpike in 1840 as closely as you can. Which present-day highway is on this route? _____

3. Which present-day highway follows about the same route as the Mohawk Turnpike and Seneca Road did in 1840? _____

Harcourt Brace School Publishers

Transportation in Your Community

DIRECTIONS: Think about the kinds of transportation that people use in your community. Then fill in the chart below.

Bicycle	**Car**
What kind? _____	What kind? _____
Where does it take you?	Where does it take you?
_____	_____
_____	_____
When is a bicycle a good transportation choice?	When is a car a good transportation choice?
_____	_____
_____	_____
Train	**Airplane**
What kind? _____	What kind? _____
Where does it take you?	Where does it take you?
_____	_____
_____	_____
When is a train a good transportation choice?	When is an airplane a good transportation choice?
_____	_____
_____	_____
Boat	**Bus**
What kind? _____	What kind? _____
Where does it take you?	Where does it take you?
_____	_____
_____	_____
When is a boat a good transportation choice?	When is a bus a good transportation choice?
_____	_____
_____	_____

Harcourt Brace School Publishers

Immigrants Arrive

The United States has always been a nation of immigrants. Most come to make a better life. The early immigrants to North American colonies arrived mainly from Britain and the Netherlands.

Around 1830, new groups of immigrants started to arrive from other parts of Europe. Many of these people could not speak English, and some were very poor.

In 1845 immigration from Ireland increased. Disease destroyed most of the potato crop that provided the main food source for many Irish people causing a **famine**, or a widespread shortage of food. About 1 million people died of starvation and from diseases their bodies were too weak to fight off.

Many who survived bought a boat ticket to the United States. Between 1845 and 1855 about 1.5 million Irish immigrants arrived in the United States. By 1890 New York City had twice as many Irish people as the largest city in Ireland.

In the 1890s thousands of Italian, Russian, and Polish people came to New York seeking a new life. These immigrants brought their culture—language, foods, clothing, music, customs, holidays, and religions—with them.

Throughout the 1800s immigration continued to rise. Between 1901 and 1910 almost 9 million more people came to the United States.

Immigrants in New York Harbor in the mid-1800s

Review

CHECK UNDERSTANDING

1. How were the immigrants who arrived in the 1800s different from those who had arrived in the colonial period?
2. What was the main cause of Irish immigration in the 1800s?

THINK CRITICALLY

3. How do you think the different cultures of new immigrants affected the American identity?

SHOW WHAT YOU KNOW

Imagine that you are packing a single suitcase to move to another country far across the ocean. Write a paragraph describing what you would bring and telling why the things you chose are important to you.

Harcourt Brace School Publishers

Activity

New Yorkers, Slavery, and the Civil War

DIRECTIONS: Read the paragraphs below. Then copy and complete the cause-and-effect chart on a separate sheet of paper.

Slavery in North America was a topic that had divided Americans since colonial times. Even before the American Revolution, many New Yorkers and other colonists felt that owning slaves was wrong. The movement started by people who wanted to end slavery is known as **abolitionism** (a•bul•LIH•shuhn•izm). Many New Yorkers were abolitionists. In fact, New York State abolished, or ended, slavery in 1827. It would be 36 years before slavery ended throughout the United States.

Some of the most famous New York abolitionists had been slaves themselves. Frederick Douglass was a former slave. He started an anti-slavery newspaper in Rochester, New York. Douglass's paper was called the *North Star* because escaped slaves from the south could use the North Star to guide them to freedom.

In 1861 the Civil War began. A **civil war** is a war between people of the same country. The United States Civil War was fought between people living in Northern and Southern states. A main cause of the war was the question of slavery. Most people in the **Union**, or North, wanted to end slavery. In the South people wanted to keep it because they believed slaves were needed to work on farms.

In 1863 Congress passed a law that required young men to join the Union army. The law was called a draft law. All men between the ages of 20 and 45 years had to serve in the army unless they could pay a $300 fee. Many people living in New York City could not afford to pay the fee. Hundreds of people took to the streets to object to the law. These draft riots lasted four days. In the end, New Yorkers from all backgrounds did join the Union Army.

The Civil War lasted from 1861 to 1865. More Americans were killed in this war than in any other United States war. No state in the North gave more money, soldiers, supplies, or support to the Union cause than New York did. At war's end nearly 500,000 New Yorkers had fought in the Union Army. The North won the war, and slavery was no longer allowed in the United States.

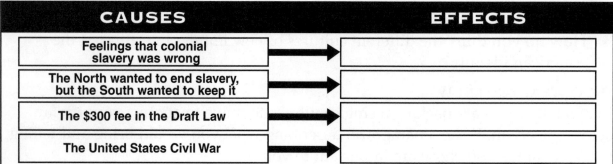

CAUSES	EFFECTS
Feelings that colonial slavery was wrong	
The North wanted to end slavery, but the South wanted to keep it	
The $300 fee in the Draft Law	
The United States Civil War	

Harcourt Brace School Publishers

Immigrant Contributions

DIRECTIONS: *Study the table of people who immigrated to the United States. Then answer the questions.*

NAME (BORN–DIED)	PLACE IMMIGRATED FROM	DATE ARRIVED IN THE U.S.	ACHIEVEMENTS
Madeleine Albright (1937–)	Czechoslovakia (now the countries of Czech Republic and Slovakia)	1948	First female to be appointed secretary of state of the United States
Julia Alvarez (1950–)	Dominican Republic	1960	Novelist who wrote the novel *How the Garcia Girls Lost Their Accents*
Isaac Asimov* (1920–1992)	Russia	1923	Science fiction writer who wrote "I, Robot" and other stories
Mikhail Baryshnikov (1948–)	Russia	1974	Dancer who performed with the New York City Ballet
Irving Berlin* (1888–1989)	Russia	1893	Composer who wrote the song "God Bless America"
Mother Frances Cabrini (1850–1917)	Italy	1889	Catholic missionary who founded schools and charities serving the poor people of New York
Bela Lugosi* (1884–1956)	Romania	1921	Actor who played Dracula on stage and screen
Hakeem Olajuwon (1963–)	Nigeria	1980	NBA star basketball player

*Entered through Ellis Island in New York

1. According to the table, which person was the youngest to come to the United States? Where did he or she come from, and at what age?

_____

2. Which country did the most people listed in the table come from?

_____

3. How many people listed in the table arrived before 1900? _____

4. How many people listed in the table went into some form of entertainment?

Who were they? _____

Harcourt Brace School Publishers

Activity

New York: Our Nation's Front Door

DIRECTIONS: Read the paragraph below, and study the map. Then complete the activities that follow.

Every place has an **absolute location**, or an exact position on Earth. Mapmakers use a system of imaginary crossed lines to show absolute locations. Lines that run east and west on a map are called lines of latitude (LA•tuh•tood). Lines that run north and south on a map are called lines of longitude (LAHN•juh•tood). Together, these lines form a grid that can locate any place.

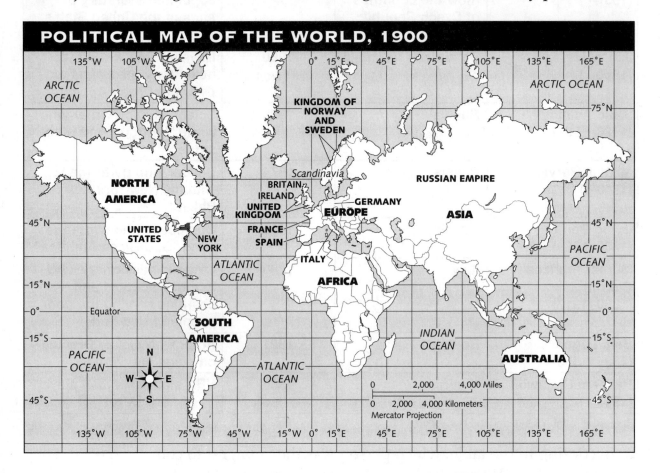

POLITICAL MAP OF THE WORLD, 1900

1. Find New York on the map. Which lines of latitude and longitude are nearest New York? ———— latitude ———— longitude

2. Use a map of New York State with a grid to find the exact location of your community. ———— latitude ———— longitude

3. In the ten-year period between 1890 and 1900, most immigrants came from the following places: Britain, Ireland, Germany, France, Italy, Spain, Russia, and Scandinavia. On the map, draw lines from those places to New York. You may want to use different colored pencils for each line.

Harcourt Brace School Publishers

Examine Text and Visuals

Ellis Island

In 1890 the United States decided to keep track of the large numbers of people entering the country. To do this, the federal government built an immigration office on Ellis Island in New York Harbor. The office opened on January 1, 1892. Immigrants crowded into a huge registration hall where they sat waiting for doctors to examine them and clerks to interview them.

Photograph A below shows the registration hall as it looked in 1892. Photograph B shows the same hall in 1951. The new design was planned to make the hall more friendly and useful.

Photograph A: Registration Hall, 1892

Photograph B: Registration Hall, 1951

DIRECTIONS: Use the graphic organizer below to compare and contrast the registration hall in 1892 and 1951.

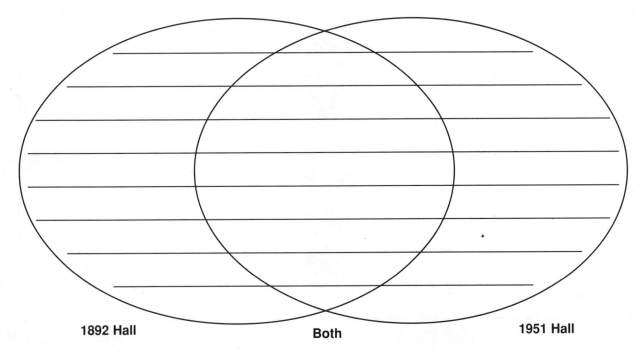

1892 Hall   **Both**   **1951 Hall**

Harcourt Brace School Publishers

Trace Your Community's History

DIRECTIONS: Use the library or the Internet to find out about important events that occurred in your community's history. Mark the time line below with dates, and describe at least three important events from your community's history.

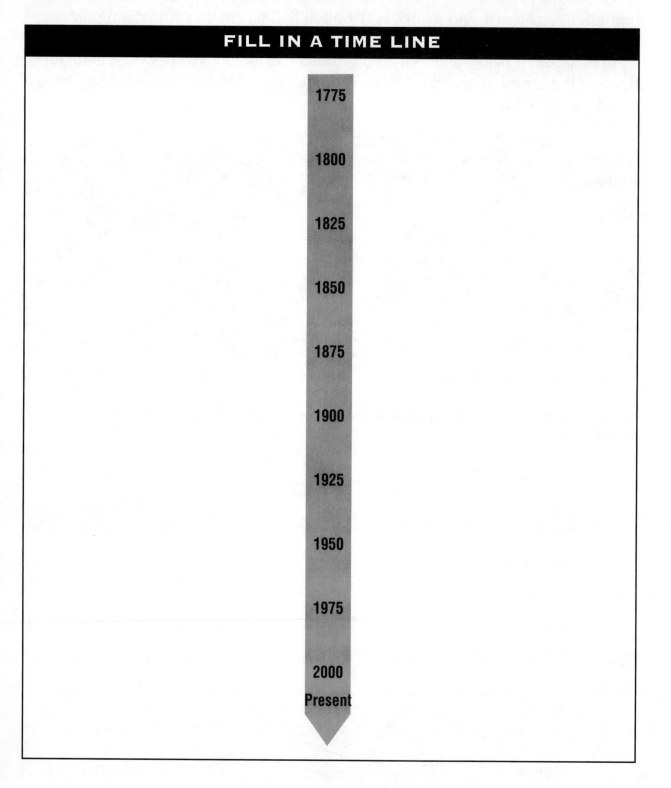

FILL IN A TIME LINE

1775

1800

1825

1850

1875

1900

1925

1950

1975

2000

Present

Harcourt Brace School Publishers

The Growth of Cities

Beginning in the 1800s New York was one of the country's leaders in manufacturing. Cities such as Rochester, Albany, Troy, Rome, and Utica manufactured a wide variety of products for homes and industries. New York City became the nation's leading clothes-making center.

Population in cities grew with the factories. Workers came from rural areas and across the sea. By 1890 New York City had more than 2.5 million people. Four out of ten workers were immigrants. Thousands of newcomers crowded into the Lower East Side of New York City. These people formed communities with the customs, foods, and languages of distant countries. Many New York workers lived in small apartments, or **tenements.**

New Yorkers built parks for quiet and clean places to go. The most famous of the public parks, Central Park in New York City, opened in the 1860s.

In more crowded areas of the cities, tall buildings called skyscrapers began to rise. The invention of the safety

Tenement room in New York City, 1890s

elevator in 1857 by Elisha Otis, in Yonkers, made these new buildings possible. The first true skyscraper rose in New York City in 1887, with 13 stories.

Many African Americans moved into New York City to work in the factories. One area, called Harlem, had about 50,000 African American residents in the 1920s. Harlem also drew many African American artists, musicians, and writers. It became a cultural center for African Americans in New York State and across the United States. This period of growth in the African American culture is remembered as the Harlem Renaissance (REH•nuh•sahns).

Review

CHECK UNDERSTANDING

1. Which cities helped make New York State a leading manufacturing center?
2. What were some ways immigrants made city life like life in their homeland?

THINK CRITICALLY

3. Why do you think the invention of the elevator changed city life?

SHOW WHAT YOU KNOW

Many inventions in the 1800s and 1900s changed the way people lived. Think about the machines that you use today. Write a paragraph describing what you think is the most important invention since the Industrial Revolution. Be sure you tell why you chose that invention and what you imagine life might be like without it.

Harcourt Brace School Publishers

Child Labor in New York

DIRECTIONS: *Read the following paragraphs about child labor. Imagine that you are living during this time. On a separate sheet of paper, write a letter to President Theodore Roosevelt telling him why you think child labor laws are important. Also explain what kinds of things these laws should include.*

During the late 1800s and early 1900s, American children between six and fifteen years old often worked at full-time jobs. Around 1900 almost 300,000 of them were working in mills, mines, and factories. Many of those jobs were dangerous. Thousands more children labored on city streets, polishing shoes or selling newspapers, flowers, or candy. These children had to work to help support their families. They were not able to go to school.

In 1903 a 73-year-old activist for workers' rights, Mary Jones, also known as Mother Jones, made a stop in Kensington, Pennsylvania. She came to help organize a protest with 75,000 textile workers demanding higher pay and shorter hours. Mother Jones realized that at least 10,000 of these workers were children. Some had lost fingers, thumbs, and whole hands in the machines at their factories.

To protest what she called "the crime of child labor," Mother Jones led the children on a march across New Jersey and New York. They were going to President Theodore Roosevelt's home in Oyster Bay, Long Island. The protesters carried banners that said "We want time to play." When Mother Jones and the children reached Oyster Bay, the President refused to see them.

The march caught the attention of reporters and made national newspaper headlines. Soon the whole country was reading about the child labor problem. Still the Congress did not pass a law to protect children in the workplace until 1938.

Children worked as newspaper sellers on the streets of New York City. Above, two children stand in front of City Hall in 1896.

Harcourt Brace School Publishers

Changes in New York Schools

DIRECTIONS: *Below is an attendance sheet and lesson plan. It is from an 1849 classroom in Cayuga County, New York. Students had to complete their lessons in order from 1–8. Sometimes they had to repeat a lesson. Use clues from the document to complete the chart comparing New York schools before 1860 and New York schools after 1860.*

1849 DISTRICT NO. 13																			
age . ☞		7	13	11	13	9	8	18	10	9	7	13	10	6			20		
Monday,	Jan. 1																		
Tuesday,	2				1	1	1	1		1	1								
Wednesday,	3				2	2	2	2	1	2	2								
Thursday,	4	1			3	3	3	3	2	3	3								
Friday,	5				4	4	3	3	3	4	4								
Saturday,	6				5	5	4	4	4	5	5								
Monday,	8	1	1		6	6	4	5	5	6	6								
Tuesday,	9	2	2		7	7	5	6	6	6	7								
Wednesday,	10	3	2		8	8	6	7	7	6	8								

Students in New York Schools

Before 1860	After 1860
1.	were divided into grades based on age
2.	met Monday through Friday
3.	had to attend class regularly
4	studied the same lesson at the same time
5.	were separated into two classrooms, one for boys and one for girls

Harcourt Brace School Publishers

Examine Text and Visuals

Schoolbooks in the 1800s

DIRECTIONS: Examine the two pages from old schoolbooks. Then support each statement below with at least one detail from the pages.

24   THE NATIONAL

Selling Goods at Auction to the Highest Bidder.

LESSON XVII.—*Words of two syllables.*

ab ba	po et	do er	ex it	bo ny
au na	su et	dy er	ed it	po ny
he ro	so da	li on	ju ry	po sy
ze ro	so fa	ci on	fu ry	ro sy
di al	du el	ha lo	ma ry	ha zy
vi al	fu el	so lo	va ry	ma zy

Omnibus, Driver, Trees, Street, Bowling Green.

If a-ny of the boys or girls who read this book should ev-er go in-to Broad-way, New-York, they will see a great ma-ny kinds of coach-es. Some are like those in the pic-ture. The dri-ver cries, " Ride up !" or " Ride down !" and the men and wom-en get in, and are ta-ken as far as they want to go. The pic-ture shows one just start-ing up from " Bowl-ing Green," in Broad-way. It is full of pas-sen-gers, and oth-ers must wait till the next one comes. Have pa-tience ; it will be here in five min-utes or less.

Book A, 1845 to 1855

LESSON XXX.   **33**

The people of the United States are famous for perseverance and inventive genius. A few years ago, people rode in stage-coaches over rough and hilly roads ; but now they travel by steamboat or railroad.

A STEAMBOAT is moved along by the two large wheels revolving in the water. The wheels are moved by STEAM, which rises from boiling water. Traveling by steamboat began about sixty years ago ; and by railroad, about forty years ago.

A STEAMSHIP differs from a Steamboat in having sails besides the steam power. A SAILING VESSEL is moved by the wind blowing against the sails.

The TELEGRAPH you see in the picture is a long iron wire supported by tall poles. At each end of the wire there is an instrument, by which men send messages with lightning velocity. The telegraph was invented by Prof. Morse, about thirty years ago.

Book B, 1876

1. Some words used in schoolbooks of the 1800s are unfamiliar today.

_____

2. Transportation was an important topic in schoolbooks of the 1800s.

_____

3. Traveling by train was more common in the 1870s than in the 1840s.

_____

4. Communication improved between the 1840s and 1870s.

_____

Harcourt Brace School Publishers

Unit 5 Practice Test

PART I: MULTIPLE-CHOICE

DIRECTIONS: (Questions 1–10) Choose the best answer to each question or incomplete statement. Circle the letter of the answer you choose.

1. Robert Fulton is best known for building a

   A canal.

   C stagecoach.

   B railroad.

   D steamboat.

2. The Erie Canal connected Lake Erie and

   A the Chesapeake Bay.

   C Lake Ontario.

   B the Hudson River.

   D the Ohio River.

3. Who invented the telegraph?

   A Samuel Morse

   C Robert Livingston

   B Peter Cooper

   D Elias Howe

4. In the 1800s, the largest number of immigrants came to the United States from

   A Africa.

   C Europe.

   B Asia.

   D Australia.

5. Why did so many Irish immigrants come to the United States between 1845 and 1855?

   A They wanted to escape from a war in Ireland.

   C They were seeking religious freedom.

   B Disease destroyed most of the potato crop in Ireland.

   D They wanted to learn to speak English.

6. The main cause of the Civil War was a disagreement over

   A slavery and states rights.

   C religion and politics.

   B taxes and representation.

   D trade and taxes.

Harcourt Brace School Publishers

7. Beginning in 1892, most immigrants who came to the east coast of the United States first landed at

    A Staten Island.

    C Coney Island.

    B Long Island.

    D Ellis Island.

8. When Mother Jones led protests in the early 1900s, her main goal was to

    A end the drafting of young men into the army.

    C improve working conditions for laborers, especially children.

    B increase the number of immigrants to the United States.

    D win the right for women to vote in elections.

Use the table below to answer Questions 9–10.

POPULATION OF CITIES: 1850–1900

City	Population in 1850	Population in 1900
Buffalo, New York	42,261	352,387
Newark, New Jersey	38,894	246,070
New York City, New York	696,115	3,437,202
Rochester, New York	36,403	162,608

9. Which city had the largest population in 1850?

    A Buffalo

    C Rochester

    B New York City

    D Newark

10. Which of the following conclusions can be drawn from the information in the table?

    A Most people living in these cities were immigrants from Ireland.

    C By 1900 the largest of these four cities was Newark.

    B The population of Rochester increased because of manufacturing.

    D The population of all four cities grew rapidly from 1850 to 1900.

Harcourt Brace School Publishers

PART II: CONSTRUCTED RESPONSE ITEMS

DIRECTIONS: (Questions 11–20) Write your answer to each question on the lines provided.
(2 points each)

For Questions 11–12, read the time line below.

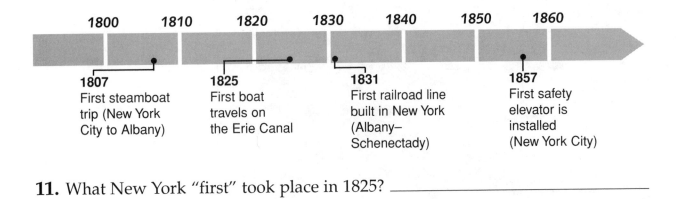

11. What New York "first" took place in 1825? _____

_____

12. Choose one of the events on the time line and explain how it helped bring

about change in New York State. _____

For Questions 13–15, use the graph below.

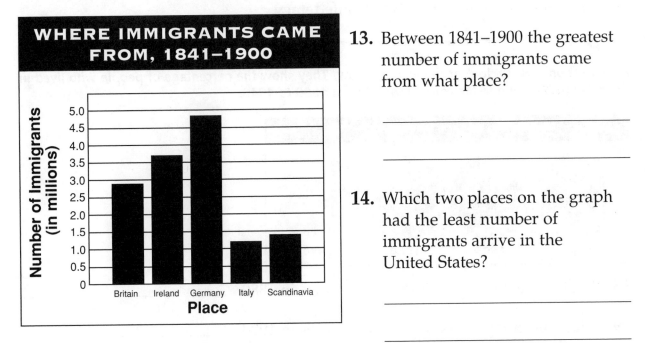

13. Between 1841–1900 the greatest
number of immigrants came
from what place?

_____

_____

14. Which two places on the graph
had the least number of
immigrants arrive in the
United States?

_____

_____

15. From 1841 to 1900, about how many immigrants came to the United States

from Britain? _____

Harcourt Brace School Publishers

For Questions 16–18, use the map below. It shows the division of states between the Union (North) and the Confederacy (South) during the Civil War.

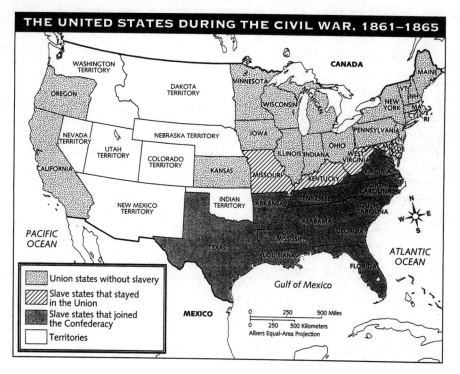

THE UNITED STATES DURING THE CIVIL WAR, 1861–1865

Union states without slavery
Slave states that stayed in the Union
Slave states that joined the Confederacy
Territories

16. List three states in the Union that did not have slavery.

_____

17. List three states that joined the Confederacy.

_____

For Questions 18–20, look at the graphs below. They show the percentage of people who lived in the cities (urban) and in the country (rural) from 1880 to 1940.

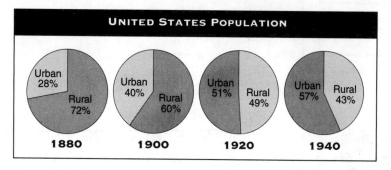

UNITED STATES POPULATION

Urban 28% Rural 72% **1880**
Urban 40% Rural 60% **1900**
Urban 51% Rural 49% **1920**
Urban 57% Rural 43% **1940**

18. What percentage of people lived in cities in 1880? _____

19. What percentage of people lived in cities in 1920? _____

20. According to these graphs, what major change in the U.S. population took

place between 1880 and 1940? _____

_____

Harcourt Brace School Publishers

PART III: DOCUMENT-BASED QUESTIONS

DIRECTIONS: *This part of the test is designed to find out how well you think and write in social studies.*

Historical Background: Between 1870 and 1900, enormous changes took place in the United States. The country grew in population and became a worldwide leader of industry. Few places showed the effects of these changes more clearly than New York City.

Below are three photographs taken around 1900. The first features the Chelsea Telephone Exchange, a central telephone terminal for New York City phone calls. The second shows a crowded street in New York City. The third pictures a group of immigrants arriving in New York's Ellis Island.

Task: Write an essay about life in New York City in the late 1800s. In your essay describe some of the major changes that took place in New York City from 1870 to 1900. Use the photographs and the answers you give in Part A to help you write your essay.

PART A: SHORT ANSWER

Look at each photograph, read the captions, and answer the questions that follow.

Photograph 1: The Chelsea Telephone Exchange

Dozens of operators transferred thousands of phone calls every hour in a central telephone terminal. The new invention of the telephone allowed people to communicate instantly over great distances for the first time.

What does this photograph suggest about the popularity of the telephone?

_____

_____

How did the telephone affect the way people communicated over distances?

_____

_____

Harcourt Brace School Publishers

Photograph 2: Traffic Jam

By 1900 the streets of New York City were lit by electric lights, filled with trolleys, and jammed with traffic. New Yorkers tried to help solve the traffic problem by building elevated railway tracks.

What inventions do you see in this photo that you would not have seen in a photo of New York City before 1850?

_____

_____

What changes in city life does this picture

suggest? _____

_____

Photograph 3: New Arrivals

In 1850 the population of New York City was close to 700,000 people. By 1900 it had grown to nearly 3.5 million. Many of the newcomers were immigrants who came from many different countries and spoke dozens of different languages.

How did the population of New York City change from 1850 to 1900?

_____

Why might you have heard different languages spoken in New York City if you

visited there in 1900? _____

PART B: ESSAY RESPONSE

On a separate sheet of paper, write an essay about life in New York City in the late 1800s. Use the documents and the answers you gave in Part A to help you plan your essay.

In your essay, remember to:

- Explain how new inventions changed life in New York.
- Identify ways in which the city itself was affected by new technologies
- Describe how cities changed due to large numbers of immigrants

Harcourt Brace School Publishers

Democracy in the United States

The United States has a government made up of its citizens. **Citizens** are the members of a town or city, a state, or a country. A government in which the citizens make the decisions is a **democracy** (dih•MAHK•ruh•see). The writers of the United States Constitution wanted to form a government that gave people a voice in making decisions.

Although the United States is a democracy, not every citizen votes on every law. Instead, the United States has a **representative democracy.** This means that citizens, including those living in New York State, vote for people to represent them in the government. Leaders are elected to run the national, state, and local governments.

Representatives elected to the United States Congress make laws and other decisions for those they represent. Americans expect their representatives to work for everyone's best interests. They are supposed to create laws and make decisions that are for the common good.

In a democracy not everyone needs to agree. All that is needed is the agreement of the **majority,** or more than half, of the citizens. Under the Constitution a person's freedom to disagree with the majority is protected. All citizens are allowed to think and say what they want to, without worrying that they may be breaking the law.

The American flag, a symbol of democracy in the United States

Americans count on their government to protect their rights. One part of the United States Constitution is called the Bill of Rights. The Bill of Rights protects the basic freedoms of United States citizens—freedoms of religion, speech, the press, peaceful gathering, privacy, and due process (the right to a fair trial).

Every law made by the Congress must maintain these rights. If representatives ignore some people's rights and pass unfair laws, voters can elect new representatives.

Review

CHECK UNDERSTANDING

1. What kind of government does the United States have?
2. What freedoms are protected by the Bill of Rights?

THINK CRITICALLY

3. Why do you think it is important that governments work for the common good?

SHOW WHAT YOU KNOW

The American flag is one of many symbols of American democracy. Design a flyer that shows other symbols that you think stand for democracy in the United States.

Harcourt Brace School Publishers

Activity

Branches of the United States Government

The Constitution has provided for three **branches,** or parts, to the federal government: the executive (ig•ZEK•yuh•tiv) branch, the legislative (LEJ•uhs•lay•tiv) branch, and the judicial (ju•DIH•shuhl) branch. Each part has a separate job to do. The three branches work together. At the same time, each branch keeps watch on the other two. That way, no one branch can become too powerful.

Executive Branch: The President with the Cabinet and law enforcement departments	• Carries out laws • Suggests new laws • Can **veto,** or cancel, a law passed by Congress • Represents the country as chief of state • Is commander in chief of the armed forces
Legislative Branch: Congress— The House of Representatives and the Senate	• Makes laws • Creates departments and programs • Approves the federal budget • May impeach and remove elected officials • Approves treaties (Senate only) • May cancel a presidential veto if two-thirds of both houses approve.
Judicial Branch: Supreme Court and other federal courts	• Decides cases that test laws to see if they are legal under the Constitution • Decides cases involving federal laws and treaties • Decides cases involving citizens who live in different states

DIRECTIONS: Read each statement below. If the power listed belongs to the executive branch, write EB on the blank line. If the power belongs to the legislative branch, write LB. If the power belongs to the judicial branch, write JB.

_____ **1.** Can recommend a new law to Congress

_____ **2.** Can veto a bill passed by Congress

_____ **3.** Hears cases involving citizens from different states

_____ **4.** Makes laws

_____ **5.** Approves treaties

_____ **6.** Can cancel a presidential veto if two-thirds of its members approve

_____ **7.** Approves the federal budget

_____ **8.** Interprets the laws

Harcourt Brace School Publishers

Examine Text and Visuals

Patriotic Songs

Americans have written many patriotic songs telling of their love for their country. The words to two famous American patriotic songs are printed below.

The Star-Spangled Banner
Written by Francis Scott Key (1814)

Oh, say can you see by the dawn's
   early light
What so proudly we hail'd at the
   twilight's last gleaming,
Whose broad stripes and bright stars
   through the perilous fight
O'er the ramparts we watch'd were so
   gallantly streaming?
And the rockets' red glare, the bombs
   bursting in air,
Gave proof through the night that our
   flag was still there.
Oh, say does that star-spangled banner
   yet wave
O'er the land of the free and the home
   of the brave?

You're a Grand Old Flag
Music and Lyrics: George M. Cohan (1906)

You're a Grand Old Flag
You're a High Flying Flag
And forever, in peace, may you wave!
You're the emblem of the land I love,
The home of the free and the brave!

Ev'ry heart beats true 'neath the
   Red, White, and Blue,
Where there's never a boast or a brag.
But should [old] acquaintance be forgot
Keep your eye on the Grand Old Flag!

DIRECTIONS: Fill in the chart below about the two patriotic songs. Then on a separate sheet of paper, write a paragraph comparing and contrasting the two songs.

	The Star-Spangled Banner	*You're a Grand Old Flag*
Subject of Song		
Some Patriotic Words in Song		
Purpose of Song		

Harcourt Brace School Publishers

New Yorkers in the National Government

DIRECTIONS: Use an almanac or a government Web site to find out about representatives in the national government from New York and from your community or district. Use this information to fill in the chart.

UNITED STATES SENATE SENATOR 1	
Name	
Political Party	
Hometown	
Year Elected	

SENATOR 2	
Name	
Political Party	
Hometown	
Year Elected	

UNITED STATES HOUSE REPRESENTATIVE	
District	
Political Party	
Name	
Hometown	
Year Elected	

Harcourt Brace School Publishers

State Government in New York

Most state governments, including that of New York, are similar to the national government. The main purpose of state governments is to make and enforce laws for the common good of that state.

The executive branch of New York's state government enforces state laws. Every four years, voters in New York elect a **governor,** or the head of the state's executive branch. At the same time, voters elect a **lieutenant governor,** who works with the governor and may serve as governor under special conditions. New York voters also elect several other officials of the executive branch. The **attorney general** acts as the state's lawyer. The **comptroller** watches where state money is spent.

The legislative branch makes state laws. This branch has two houses, or parts, a senate and an assembly. Together they are known as the **legislature.** The senate has 61 members. The assembly has 150 members. Voters elect representatives to both houses every two years.

Both houses of the legislature can suggest new laws for New York. An idea for a new law is called a **bill.** A bill must be approved in both houses and signed by the governor before it becomes a law.

New York's state courts make up its **judicial branch.** The most powerful court in the state is the Court of Appeals. The chief justice and six other justices serve on this court for 14-year periods. The Court of Appeals reviews cases sent to it by lower courts. These include a supreme court that is divided into four sections. There are a total of 24 justices for the four sections of the New York Supreme Court. They serve for five-year periods.

New York State capitol building in Albany

Review

CHECK UNDERSTANDING

1. What is the job title of the chief executive of New York State?
2. What are the two parts of the New York state legislative branch?

THINK CRITICALLY

3. Why do you think New York state government is similar to the national government?

SHOW WHAT YOU KNOW

On a separate sheet of paper, create an idea web with a center labeled *New York State Government.* Draw and label three sections for each of the three branches of government. Then complete the web with details about each branch.

Harcourt Brace School Publishers

How a Bill Becomes a Law in New York

DIRECTIONS: *Study the chart below. Put a **T** by statements that are true and an **F** by statements that are false.*

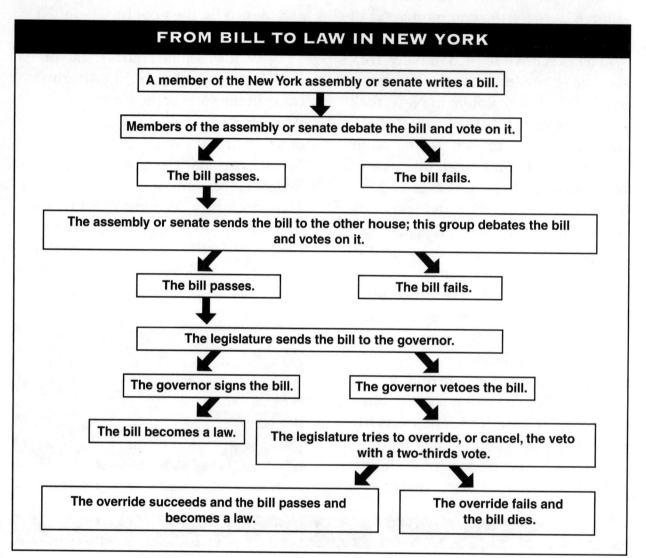

FROM BILL TO LAW IN NEW YORK

A member of the New York assembly or senate writes a bill.

Members of the assembly or senate debate the bill and vote on it.

The bill passes.

The bill fails.

The assembly or senate sends the bill to the other house; this group debates the bill and votes on it.

The bill passes.

The bill fails.

The legislature sends the bill to the governor.

The governor signs the bill.

The governor vetoes the bill.

The bill becomes a law.

The legislature tries to override, or cancel, the veto with a two-thirds vote.

The override succeeds and the bill passes and becomes a law.

The override fails and the bill dies.

_____ **1.** In New York, only the senate can introduce bills.

_____ **2.** Both the assembly and the senate debate a bill before it becomes law.

_____ **3.** Once the governor vetoes a bill, it cannot become a law.

_____ **4.** The legislature can override the governor's veto.

_____ **5.** When an override fails, a bill becomes a law.

_____ **6.** The governor can write a bill.

Harcourt Brace School Publishers

Activity

State Symbols

Each of the 50 states of the United States has several symbols that stand for its history and culture. These symbols range from flags to flowers to birds. New York has each of these, as well as a state gem, a state fruit, a state tree, and even a state fossil. All symbols have to be approved by the legislature to be adopted by the state.

	NEW YORK STATE SYMBOLS		
Symbol	**Name and Picture**	**Date Adopted**	**Reason for Adopting the Symbol**
State flower	rose	1955	Roses are found in many gardens across the state.
State tree	sugar maple	1956	Many sugar maple trees grow in New York. They have pointed leaves that change color in the fall and sap that is used to make maple syrup.
State animal	beaver	1975	New York has a long history of fur trade, especially trade in beaver furs. Europeans settled in the Albany area to trade for beaver furs with Native Americans.
State fish	brook trout	1975	Brook trout live in hundreds of lakes, rivers, and ponds in New York.
State gem	garnet	1969	New York has the largest garnet mine in the world. This mine is the Barton Mine in the Adirondack Mountains.
State bird	red-breasted bluebird	1970	This bird has made a comeback in New York after nearly disappearing in the 1950s. Many people provide nesting boxes for red-breasted bluebirds in the winter.
State fruit	apple	1976	Many kinds of apples grow in New York State.
State fossil	*Eurypterus remipes*	1984	An extinct relative of the modern king crab and the sea scorpion, this creature lived in the sea that once covered most of New York.

Harcourt Brace School Publishers

(continued)

DIRECTIONS: *Create your own state symbol. Tell why your symbol is a good one for New York State.*

My Symbol

My symbol is a good one for New York State because:

_____

_____

_____

_____

_____

_____

_____

Harcourt Brace School Publishers

The New York State Flag

One of New York's most important symbols is the state seal, which is used on all official state papers. The seal also appears on the state flag.

On the center of the seal is a gold shield. The shield shows two ships sailing on a river. In the background the sun shines brightly above the mountains. On top of the shield, an American eagle stands on a globe to represent the European settlement of North America.

The figure at the left of the shield represents liberty. She holds a pole with a Liberty cap on it. On the New York flag, the cap stands for freedom. At Liberty's feet is a crown that symbolizes the American colonists' defeat of the British in the American Revolution.

The figure of Justice stands at the right. Her sword stands for the swift and strong nature of justice. The blindfold and the scales show that justice does not favor anyone but treats all people fairly.

The word, *Excelsior* (ik•SEL•see•er), is the state motto. It means "Ever Upward" and was chosen to remind people to aim higher.

DIRECTIONS: Color the New York State flag, using the flag on the cover of this book as a guide. Then, in your own words, write a brief description of the meaning of the seal that appears on the flag.

Harcourt Brace School Publishers

Your Community

Who Represents You in State Government?

DIRECTIONS: Use the library or the Internet to find information about your governor, state senator, and state representative. Use the information you find to fill in the charts below.

GOVERNOR	
Name	
Political Party	
Hometown	
Year Elected	

STATE SENATOR	
District	
Name	
Political Party	
Hometown	
Year Elected	

GENERAL ASSEMBLY MEMBER	
District	
Name	
Political Party	
Hometown	
Year Elected	

Harcourt Brace School Publishers

Local Government

New York State has three levels of local government. The three levels are county, city or town, and village. Local governments provide services and make laws for communities. They also maintain police and fire departments.

County governments provide services to their communities. Today, county governments are providing more services than ever before. Some county governments maintain hospitals, courts, jails, and highways. In every county there is a courthouse where local court cases are decided. New York's county governments are headed by an elected board of county supervisors or a legislature.

The second level of local government is that of the cities and towns. Most cities in New York State are governed by an elected mayor and council. The main job of the mayor is to run the city council and choose people for different offices, or jobs.

A few cities have a city manager, instead of a mayor. This person is

Courthouse in Ontario County, New York

picked by the city council. The city manager acts as a supervisor for work in all the main departments and reports to the council. Some cities need both an elected mayor and a city manager.

Town governments are much like those of cities. Usually a town is run by a town manager or supervisor, but a town may have a mayor.

The third level of local government takes place in a village, which is usually a part of a town. Village governments provide services to smaller numbers of people.

Review

CHECK UNDERSTANDING

1. What are the three levels of local government in New York State?
2. What kinds of services do county governments provide?

THINK CRITICALLY

3. Why do you think New York needs both state and local governments?

SHOW WHAT YOU KNOW

Look in a local newspaper for an article telling about a service provided by your local government. Write a short summary to share with your classmates.

Harcourt Brace School Publishers

Activity

Services of County Governments

DIRECTIONS: *Some departments of the Suffolk County government on Long Island are listed in the box below. Match the clues with the right department to solve the puzzle.*

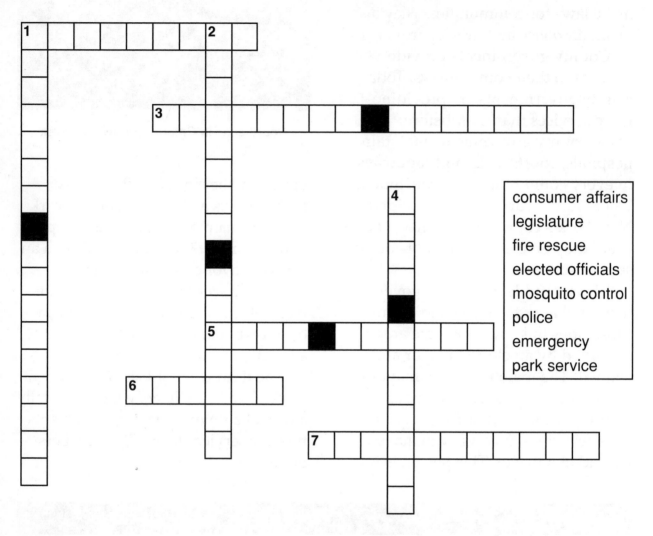

consumer affairs
legislature
fire rescue
elected officials
mosquito control
police
emergency
park service

ACROSS

1. People have been hurt in a car accident.
3. A family worries about insects in a marsh near its house.
5. An empty building catches fire.
6. Someone has stolen your bike.
7. You want to know if a certain law has been passed.

DOWN

1. You want to know who is on the board of county officials.
2. People are worried about how much they paid for something they bought.
4. Visitors to a park notice that a tree has fallen in a storm.

Harcourt Brace School Publishers

Examine Text and Visuals

A Historic Map of Counties and Townships

The map below of western New York's counties and townships is based on one that was drawn about 1825. The Holland Company bought a large amount of land from the government. The land was then sold to individuals in smaller plots, or **townships.**

Beginning in the 1780s, the New York State and national governments decided to do a **land survey,** or measure and map. Officials then divided the land into townships based on a grid system and gave them a number, known as the range. People identified the land they wished to buy by township and range number.

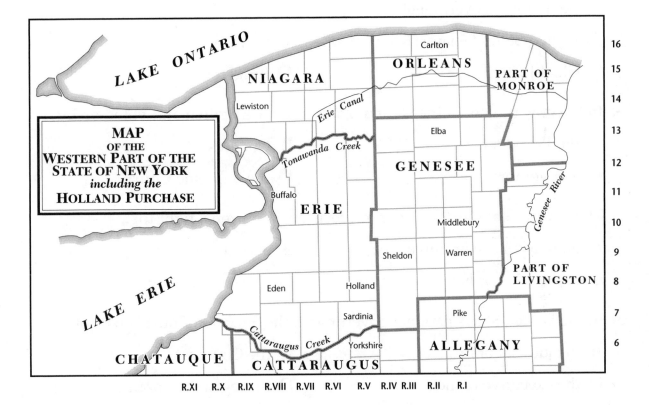

DIRECTIONS: Study the map. Then write answers to the following questions on a separate sheet of paper.

1. Which five counties have a border on one of the Great Lakes?

2. According to the map what four townships are located in Genesee County?

3. What forms the border between Erie County and Cattaraugus County?

4. Choose any two townships shown on the map. What counties are they in?

5. Who do you think used this map when it was first printed?

Harcourt Brace School Publishers

Unit 6 Practice Test

PART I: MULTIPLE-CHOICE

DIRECTIONS: (Questions 1–10) *Choose the best answer to each question or incomplete statement. Circle the letter of the answer you choose.*

1. A democracy is a government ruled by

   A a king.

   C soldiers.

   B judges.

   D the people.

2. Which of the following office holders represents the people of New York State in the national government?

   A United States Senator

   C Chief Justice

   B Governor

   D Judge

3. In the government of the United States, laws are written and voted on by

   A the President.

   C a governor.

   B Congress.

   D the Supreme Court.

4. The United States Constitution protects every citizen's right to

   A go to a college or university.

   C express his or her opinions.

   B earn money.

   D own a home.

5. In the United States national government, the Supreme Court is part of

   A the judicial branch.

   C the executive branch.

   B the Congress.

   D the legislative branch.

6. In New York's state government, the chief lawyer is the

   A governor.

   C comptroller.

   B attorney general.

   D lieutenant governor.

7. In New York, which branch of government writes and votes on state laws?

   A local

   C judicial

   B executive

   D legislative

Harcourt Brace School Publishers

8. In what way is New York's state government like the national government of the United States?

    A Its chief executive is the president.

    B Its legislature includes the Senate and the Assembly.

    C Its highest court is the Court of Appeals.

    D It has executive, legislative, and judicial branches.

For Questions 9–10, look at the chart below.

TWO LEVELS OF LOCAL GOVERNMENT

County Government	City/Town Government

Officials:
  County Supervisors
	Officials:
	  Mayor or Manager
	  City or Town Council

Services: • courts • hospitals • jails • highways • community colleges	Services: • police • firefighters • roads • public schools • trash removal

9. Which of these services is provided by city or town governments?

    A elementary schools

    B jails

    C state highways

    D courthouses

10. In most New York county governments, departments are managed by

    A councilors.

    B governors.

    C supervisors.

    D judges.

Harcourt Brace School Publishers

PART II: CONSTRUCTED RESPONSE ITEMS

DIRECTIONS: (Questions 11–20) Write your answer to each question on the lines provided.

For Questions 11–15, use the chart below. It shows the powers granted to each branch of the United States government.

Executive Branch: The President with the Cabinet and Law Enforcement Departments	• Carries out laws • Suggests new laws • Can **veto,** or cancel, a law passed by Congress • Represents the country as chief of state • Is commander in chief of the armed forces
Legislative Branch: Congress The House of Representatives and the Senate	• Makes laws • Creates departments and programs • Approves the federal budget • May impeach and remove elected officials • Approves treaties (Senate only) • May cancel a presidential veto if two-thirds of both houses approve.
Judicial Branch: Supreme Court and other Federal Courts	• Decides cases that test laws to see if they are legal under the Constitution • Decides cases involving federal laws and treaties • Decides cases involving citizens who live in different states

11. What can the President do to check, or stop, the power of Congress?

_____

12. What is the main job of the Congress?

_____

13. What is the main power of the Supreme Court?

_____

14. What branch of the government commands the armed forces?

_____

15. Which branch approves the federal budget?

_____

Harcourt Brace School Publishers

For Questions 16–18, use the chart below. It shows how a bill can become a law in New York.

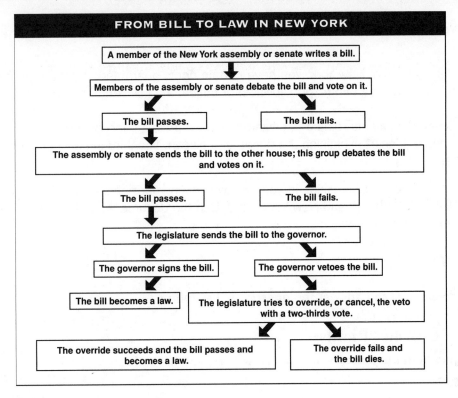

FROM BILL TO LAW IN NEW YORK

A member of the New York assembly or senate writes a bill.

Members of the assembly or senate debate the bill and vote on it.

The bill passes.

The bill fails.

The assembly or senate sends the bill to the other house; this group debates the bill and votes on it.

The bill passes.

The bill fails.

The legislature sends the bill to the governor.

The governor signs the bill.

The governor vetoes the bill.

The bill becomes a law.

The legislature tries to override, or cancel, the veto with a two-thirds vote.

The override succeeds and the bill passes and becomes a law.

The override fails and the bill dies.

16. What is the first step in making a new law? _____

_____

17. What happens just after the bill is approved in the assembly? _____

_____

18. What happens after the governor signs the bill? _____

_____

For Questions 19–20, look at the picture of the New York state seal.

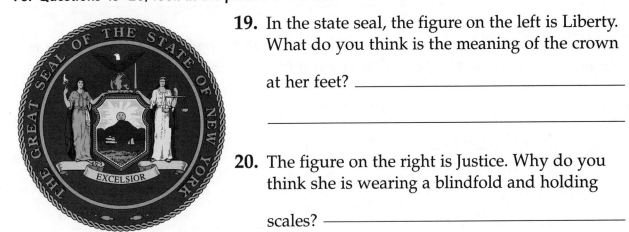

19. In the state seal, the figure on the left is Liberty. What do you think is the meaning of the crown

at her feet? _____

_____

20. The figure on the right is Justice. Why do you think she is wearing a blindfold and holding

scales? _____

_____

Harcourt Brace School Publishers

PART III: DOCUMENT-BASED QUESTIONS

Directions: This part of the test is designed to find out how well you think and write in social studies.

Background: As a citizen of New York, you have certain rights guaranteed by the New York State Constitution. You also have certain responsibilities, or duties, as a citizen of the United States of America.

Below are some documents related to citizenship. The first is a chart describing the rights of a citizen. The second is a chart explaining the duties of a citizen. The third is an illustration of a campaign poster.

Task: Write an essay about citizenship. In your essay explain your rights and responsibilities as a citizen of both the United States and New York State. Use the documents and the answers you give in Part A to help you write your essay.

PART A: SHORT ANSWER

Look at each document, and answer the questions that follow.

Document 1: Citizens' Rights

As a citizen of both the United States and New York, you have the right to:

- speak freely
- practice the religion of your choice
- practice freedom of the press
- assemble, or meet, with others peacefully
- ask the government to end an unfair practice or injustice
- have a trial by jury (if you are accused of a crime)
- vote in elections (if you are over 18 years old)

Suppose that you and some friends decided to write and print a newspaper. What right or rights are you using in this situation? _____

_____

Suppose that you go to a political meeting to support a person who is running for the state senate. What right or rights are you using?

_____

_____

Harcourt Brace School Publishers

Document 2: Citizen's Responsibilities

As a citizen of both the United States and New York State,

You Must—

- obey all national and state laws
- serve on a jury when asked
- pay taxes

- attend school (to age 16)

You Should—

- vote in elections
- serve as a witness when asked
- become involved in community activities
- become educated and stay informed

What are two things that citizens of the United States are required to do?

_____

_____

What are two things that "good" citizens should do but are not required to do?

_____

_____

Document 3: Vote for Quinn

Is the person who made this sign exercising his or her rights, his or her responsibilities, or both?

Explain. _____

_____

_____

Is a person who votes for Robert Quinn exercising his or her rights or

responsibilities, or both? Explain. _____

PART B: ESSAY RESPONSE

On a separate sheet of paper, write an essay about citizenship. In your essay explain your rights and responsibilities as a citizen of both the United States and New York State. Use the documents and the answers you gave in Part A to help you plan your essay.

In your essay, remember to:

- Explain the difference between a right and a responsibility
- Describe your rights as a citizen of the United States
- Describe your rights as a citizen of New York
- Describe your responsibilities as a citizen of the United States
- Describe your responsibilities as a citizen of New York
- Give examples of each right or responsibility

Harcourt Brace School Publishers

PHOTO CREDITS

Page Placement Key: (t)-top, (c)-center, (b)-bottom, (l)-left, (r)-right, (bg)-background.

Front Cover: (tl) Harcourt; (tr) Richard Berenholtz/The Stock Market; (cl) Alan Schein/The Stock Market; (cr) R. Kord/H. Armstrong Roberts; (bl) Richard Berenholtz/The Stock Market; (br) P. Degginger/H. Armstrong Roberts; (b)(inset) Joe McDonald/Bruce Coleman, Inc.
Back Cover: John Shaw/Bruce Coleman, Inc.

Unit 1: 21, Courtesy of the New York State Museum, Albany, NY; 22 Rochester Museum & Science Center; 27, Courtesy of the New York State Museum, Albany, NY.
Unit 2: 30 National Maritime Museum, Neg#8450; 32 The Granger Collection; 34 Collection of the New York Historical Society; 40 I. N. Phelps Stokes Collection, Miriam and Ira D. Wallach Division of Art, Prints and Photographs/The New York Public Library/Astor, Lenox and Tilden Foundations; 42 The Granger Collection.
Unit 3: 51 The Granger Collection; 53 Collection of the New York Historical Society; 63(t) The Albany Gazette, Monday, June 11, 1798. Collection of the Albany Institute of History & Art; 63(b) Culver Pictures, Inc.; 64 Picture Collection, The Branch Libraries, The New York Public Library; 65 Library of Congress; 68 Newsday, Inc; 70 Picture Collection, The Branch Libraries, The New York Public Library; 74 Library of Congress; 80 Library of Congress; 82 The Granger Collection.
Unit 4: 83 National Archives; 84 The Granger Collection; 87 Paul F. Cooper, Jr. Archives, Hartwick College, Oneonta, NY; 88(l) Allsport; 88(r) Al Bello/Allsport; 91 The Granger Collection; 92 The Granger Collection; 93 Library of Congress; 94 (detail) Collection of the New York Historical Society.
Unit 5: 103 Museum of the City of New York; 104 The Granger Collection; 105 Culver Pictures, Inc.; 109 (detail) General Research Division, The New York Public Library Astor, Lenox and Tilden Foundations; 113(l)(detail) William Williams Collection. Milstein Division of United States History, Local History and Genealogy, The New York Public Library Astor, Lenox and Tilden Foundations; 113(r)(detail) National Park Service, Statue of Liberty National Monument; 115 The Museum of the City of New York; 116(detail) Courtesy of Staten Island Historical Society; 118(l) National Pictorial Primer or First Book for Children; 118(r) First Lessons in Geography–On the Plan of Object Teaching, Designed for Beginners.
Unit 6: 123 Parks Canada/Alexander Graham Bell National Historic Site; 124(t) Archive Photos; 124(b) ©Bettmann/CORBIS; 125 Harcourt; 129 Alan Schein/The Stock Market; 133 Harcourt; 135 W. Keith McMakin; 141 One Mile Up/Harcourt.